HAUNTED HOUSES

of NEW JERSEY

HISTORY & MYSTERY IN THE GARDEN STATE

HAUNTED HOUSES of NEW JERSEY

HISTORY & MYSTERY IN THE GARDEN STATE

LYNDA LEE MACKEN

HAUNTED HOUSES OF NEW JERSEY
History & Mystery in the Garden State

Published by
Black Cat Press
P. O. Box 1218
Forked River, NJ 08731
www.lyndaleemacken.com

ISBN 978-0-9829580-6-3

Cover Design & Book Layout by Deb Tremper.
www.sixpennygraphics.com

Printed in the United States of America
by Sheridan Books, Inc.
www.sheridan.com

Contents

Introduction 1

Imlay House, Allentown 6

Stephen Crane House, Asbury Park 11

Absecon Lighthouse, Atlantic City 14

Clara Barton Schoolhouse, Bordentown 17

Emlen Physick Estate, Cape May 19

Historic Cold Spring Village, Cape May 22

Smithville Mansion, Eastampton Township 27

Union County Courthouse, Elizabeth 31

Historic Village at Allaire, Farmingdale 34

Old Schoolhouse Museum, Forked River 39

Gabreil Daveis Tavern, Glendora 42

Greenfield Hall, Haddonfield 44

Batsto Mansion, Hammonton 47

Hancock House, Hancock's Bridge 50

The Hermitage, Ho-Ho-Kus 52

River Road School, Lyndhurst 57

Mead Hall, Madison 59

Burrowes Mansion, Matawan 61

Thomas Budd House, Mount Holly 64

Acorn Hall, Morristown 67

Whitall House, National Park 69

Shippen Manor, Oxford 74

Proprietary House, Perth Amboy 77

Metlar-Bodine House, Piscataway 80

Seabrook Wilson House, Port Monmouth 82

Clarke House Museum, Princeton 87

Raritan Library, Raritan 90

Ringwood Manor, Ringwood 93

Steuben House, River Edge 97

Olde Stone House, Sewell 99

Van Wickle House, Somerset 101

Ocean County Courthouse, Toms River 104

Dey Mansion, Wayne 106

Hobart Manor, Wayne 109

Guggenheim Cottage, West Long Branch 112

Shadow Lawn, West Long Branch 114

J. Thompson Baker House, Wildwood 117

Acknowledgements 119

Bibliography 121

To those who work to preserve
the *spirit* of New Jersey.

Introduction

*"All houses wherein men have lived
and died are haunted houses."*

—HENRY WADSWORTH LONGFELLOW

A visit to New Jersey's historic houses is a step back in time, and in some cases, into another dimension. *"A dimension as vast as space and as timeless as infinity. It is the middle ground between light and shadow, between science and superstition, and it lies between the pit of man's fears and the summit of his knowledge. This is the dimension of imagination. It is an area which we call..."* the Garden State! Bet you thought I'd say *The Twilight Zone*, didn't you? And rightfully so. The above quote is one of the program's introductions penned by Rod Serling, the show's creator. Yet, I feel Serling's prologue is an apt description of alternative realities and the key to the haunting happenings at some of New Jersey's historic homes.

The scientific theory of multiple dimensions surfaced

in the 1950s, (*The Twilight Zone* first aired in1959). The co-existence of parallel worlds could account for apparitions and related paranormal phenomena. When it comes to ghosts, perhaps the person is alive and well in another realm; when they manifest in our mortal world, a corresponding universe is glimpsed.

When Jennie Tuttle Hobart's spirit gracefully glides down the staircase at Hobart Manor or Louise Schermerhorn's specter descends Acorn Hall's stairway in Morristown, their appearances may demonstrate alternative realities. A reality of higher vibration where the dearly departed continue on in the non-physical. We occasionally glimpse this sphere when ghosts invade our territory or we intrude on theirs—an overlap where our lower vibration meets their higher resonance. How it happens remains a mystery.

As a chronicler of hundreds of ghost stories over the years, I've noticed a distinct pattern. A large amount of ghostly activity occurs in hallways and on staircases. One theory suggests these highly trafficked areas hold a lot of energy and become, essentially, energy storehouses. Some speculate ghosts need to lower their vibration to materialize so they draw energy from the material realm to accomplish the astounding feat. Remarkable changes occur as an entity attempts this process. The environment cools down, hence the proverbial "cold spots." (A thermal camera can record a spirit's energetic temperature signature.) The atmosphere becomes charged with electromagnetic energy, which is why witnesses say the hairs on the back of their neck stood up. Electromagnetic field (EMF) detectors, another ghost hunting gadget, sense fluctuations in electromagnetic energy. Lights or other electronic equipment turning on and off is another example of energy manipulation by the spirit attempting to form.

Interest in the supernatural is at an all-time high— its popularity, in part, due to reality TV programs such as *Most Haunted, Ghost Hunters* and *Ghost Adventures*. New Jersey's treasure trove of historical structures is a paranormal investigator's dream. Where history exists, ghosts persist. The Atlantic Paranormal Society (TAPS) is an organization of paranormal researchers showcased on *Ghost Hunters*. Regarding the stories presented in *Haunted Houses of New Jersey*, TAPS investigated the Absecon Lighthouse, Proprietary House, Shippen Manor, Stephen Crane House and Union County Courthouse. Supernatural interest in historic sites helps keep history alive and hopefully increases revenue for underfunded heritage preservation.

The important role New Jersey played in the Revolutionary War earned the state the title of *Crossroads of the Revolution*. It's hard to imagine what people endured during the war, under constant fear of attack and looting. Emotions ran high to say the least. On both sides, neighbor alerted neighbor to the soldiers' onslaught. Ann Whitall received word from John Gill, a relative in Haddonfield, that the Hessians were coming. While quartered in Gill's house, Colonel von Donop announced his plan to capture Fort Mercer. A colonial victory ensued. Even so, some who served during the conflict still abide at Whitall's and Gill's Houses. Other Revolutionary ghosts make their homes across the state.

In the 1760s, New Jersey boasted hundreds of iron mines in its mountainous northern reaches where glaciers left the region rich in magnetite iron ore. Natural resources for iron manufacturing were there for the taking—ore for smelting, timber for fuel and water for powering equipment. Many colonial forges operated and communities developed around early furnaces. In 1742 the Shippen family (who still haunt their enterprise) built the Oxford furnace and opened local magnetite mines. The furnace in Ringwood fired up in 1762, where Peter Hasenclever, a man ahead of his time, founded the American Iron Company, a forerunner to the nation's iron and steel industry. At Ringwood Manor, the iron magnate's spirit continues to wallow in his opulent estate while James Allaire's apparition still grieves his losses at Allaire Iron Works. As the name implies, magnetite iron ore is highly magnetic. Paranormal researchers consider magnetite a prime energy source for emerging spirits and could account for inexplicable phenomena at former mining sites.

New Jersey played an integral role in the escape of slaves. It's estimated over 2,000 were on the move at one time during the most active period of the Underground Railroad. Their post-mortem presence is still sensed in some haunted homes. There is no rest for the eerie in the Burrowes Mansion and Emlen Physick Estate where faithful servants stay anchored. The Seabrook Wilson House creaks with footsteps of long dead souls and whispered secrets still echo inside its walls. Some suggest as many as 22 different ghosts dwell therein.

Readers of my *Ghosts of the Garden State* series (now out of print) may recognize some of the following stories. When those earlier books were published, (2001, 2003, 2005), obtaining information on ghosts and hauntings was like pulling teeth. Belief in ghosts was almost taboo. In fact, I recently came upon a 1987 newspaper article vehemently denying the presence of ghosts in the Thomas Budd house which is *notoriously* haunted! More than 20 credible individuals sighted full-bodied apparitions and experienced other extraordinary phenomena there. Without doubt, a shift occurred in recent years and the cultural climate changed. Ghosts have come out of the closet, so to speak. As a result, *Haunted Houses of New Jersey* presents revised stories and several new ones. Let's keep haunted history alive!

So now, dear reader, revel in the history and mystery of some of New Jersey's most welcoming haunted houses. To paraphrase General Joshua Chamberlain: *In great houses, something stays. Forms change and pass; bodies disappear; but spirits linger...*

Imlay House

28 South Main Street
Allentown

Welcome to the Imlay House! James Henderson Imlay (1764–1823) graduated Princeton College and joined the Monmouth County Militia during the Revolutionary War. As a member of the New Jersey Assembly, he served as speaker of the house in 1796. A New Jersey Congressman, he also acted as Allentown's Postmaster, the town where he resumed his law practice.

Around 1790, Imlay commissioned the exquisitely detailed mansion that bears his name. The original French wallpaper, purchased in 1794, is exhibited in the American Wing of Metropolitan Museum of Art in New York City. In addition, a replication of Imlay's sitting room is installed at Winterthur, the DuPont Estate in Wilmington, Delaware.

The building became a rooming house in 1900 and 36 years later, Dr. Walter D. Farmer converted the house into a hospital and his office where he practiced until his death. The building now holds retail shops, offices and a private residence.

Before and during the Civil War, slavery opponents assisted those seeking freedom. Allentown's concerned citizens actively aided the fugitives. In a compassionate

gesture, John Imlay accommodated runaway slaves in his home's upstairs bedrooms as opposed to the basement or other such second-rate lodging. Actually, a handmade leather shoe turned up in an upper floor hidey-hole. The material and workmanship is consistent with a 19th century slave-owned artifact and attests to their presence in the home's upper regions. This chapter in the house's history is further enhanced by the spooky story of three unearthly men playing a card game upstairs. The ghostly traces of their recreation is residual energy from the past informing the present.

Before relocating his shop called "Two Country Ducks" to Smithville, Robert Koch used to operate a retail business in the Imlay building. He said as a local television crew filmed a commercial at the site, the displeased spirits reacted to the invasion by throwing objects off the shelves. They also displaced candles and other items by moving them around from one place to another. At one time a high school girl working in the shop heard a noise in the fireplace. She approached the hearth, and thinking it might be a small animal, gently poked inside the firebox with a fireplace tool. Whoever or whatever made the sound grabbed the implement and gave it a good pull! The rattled young woman quickly exited and soon resigned.

Georgette Keenan is the long-time proprietor of "Necessities for the Heart" gift shop located in the Imlay House. She surmises many people passed away in the house because of its history of slave habitation and hospital tenancy. She says shoppers who possess psychic abilities find the store's energy intriguing and often get the "willies." One paranormally sensitive customer discerned a spirit-laden atmosphere and found it difficult to enter the back room.

When Georgette first opened her business, she presented a tea-themed shop. Working alone at night in the building she often heard clanging and banging noises coming from adjacent rooms. She said the sounds reminded her of little boys wrestling and pushing each other into walls. Growing up with two older brothers, I relate to Georgette's assessment. Georgette said this happened frequently, occurring at the same hour of night each time. She assumes the evanescent culprits are Imlay's sons whom he adored.

A spectral young woman seemed to take up residence on the porch. Passersby would sometimes spot a figure in the front window. A former shopkeeper's daughter constantly saw the phantom female darting to and fro. The wall between the porch and Georgette's shop always felt unnaturally cold. She said more than a few times as she held tea tins while showing them to customers, the container would fly out of her hand. This anomaly only occurred on the porch.

In the past, one particular vendor experienced bizarre events. During her monthly visits, the representative's computer crashed yet outside the shop the device worked perfectly. While taking inventory of the handbags the purses would plop off the shelves and fall on her head! She'd say, "Stop bothering me—you're dead!" When she at last finished scanning the merchandise for inventory purposes the computer erased all her work. Georgette and her gals often find a handbag in the *middle* of the floor. This oddity is not merely the result of pocketbooks falling off the shelf—it's too far away from the display to be a coincidence.

Twice a year, when daylight savings time began and ended, the staff needed to reset all the clocks and watches for sale in the shop. On several occasions they found this task already accomplished by unseen hands.

Office Manager, Marianne Newman, is a no nonsense kind of person. One time, as she straightened eyeglass holders displayed on a chair, Marianne spotted someone in the mirror leaning beside the chair. She turned to greet the female customer but *no one was there*.

Although the paranormal pranks petered out somewhat, Georgette feels the playful, phantoms remain. I sense the ghosts harbored in the Imlay House consider this place a safe house as did the former fugitives on their way to freedom.

Stephen Crane House

508 Fourth Avenue
Asbury Park

"A man had better think three times before he openly scorns the legends of the phantoms."
—STEPHEN CRANE

Stephen Townley Crane, born on November 1, 1871 in Newark, NJ, (Asbury Park was "born" the same year, founded by James A. Bradley) was the youngest of fourteen children. His father, Jonathan Townley Crane, served as a Methodist minister, and his mother, Mary Helen Peck, campaigned tirelessly for the Women's Christian Temperance Union.

After his father died in 1883, Crane's mother purchased "Arbutus Cottage" in Asbury Park. She enrolled her son in the public school system where he wrote his first short story. Crane later went on to work as a journalist, filing stories from Asbury Park for a New York newspaper. Crane first chronicled Garden State ghost stories in 1894 with his essay entitled "Ghosts on the Jersey Shore."

He left Asbury Park behind when in 1892 he traveled to New York City. Three years later his masterwork, *The Red Badge of Courage*, received great acclaim in America and Europe.

During an elaborate Christmas party in 1899, which lasted several days, Crane fell ill while performing a ghost story for his literary friends Joseph Conrad, Henry James and H. G. Wells, among others. He continued to write while taking the cure for tuberculosis in Germany's

Black Forest. In 1900, at the age of 28, Crane died from the disease. His remains are interred in the Evergreen Cemetery in Hillside, New Jersey. His Asbury Park address is the author's only remaining residence, his Newark birthplace razed decades ago. The home is now a museum, performance and entertainment venue hosting readings, plays and classic movies.

Many deaths and hardships occurred in Arbutus Cottage and ghostly claims run rampant. Sightings include a female apparition in the attic window and a man in Victorian clothing. It's chilling when objects move on their own in full view of dumbfounded witnesses. A fireplace trowel once flew off its rack and hit a young boy in the head. Disembodied voices are startling as is the inexplicable drop in room temperatures.

Syfy Channel's *Ghost Hunters* researched the paranormal claims. The team diligently investigated and captured some anomalies yet in the end they could neither prove nor disprove the spooky allegations. Is the Crane house haunted? Some say yes... but no one can definitely say no.

Absecon Lighthouse

31 S. Rhode Island Avenue
Atlantic City

Many wooden schooners wrecked in the coastal waters off New Jersey and these tragedies earned Absecon Inlet the nickname "Graveyard Inlet." In an effort to avert further shipwrecks, the U.S. Lighthouse Service commissioned a lighthouse on Absecon Island.

Designed by General George Meade, who also designed the Barnegat Lighthouse, the Absecon Lighthouse is the third tallest masonry lighthouse in the United States. The structure rises 171 feet skyward and a 228-step spiral staircase leads up to the lantern room which offers a panoramic view.

The fully restored lighthouse is listed on the New Jersey and National Historic Registries. The complex encompasses a light keeper's house, museum and lens exhibit.

Paranormal activity dates to 1905 when a light keeper observed the Jersey Devil atop the tower. (The Jersey Devil is a 250-year-old mythical creature said to haunt New Jersey's Pine Barrens). Over the years, dozens of wretched spirits gazed out from the lantern room over the choppy sea. Presumably, there are shipwreck victims taking refuge in the light that saved so many others from a similar fate.

Another historical specter spotted on the property is a Revolutionary War soldier who probably perished when the *Mermaid* sank in 1779. The doomed ship sailed from Halifax, Nova Scotia to New York, ran aground and wrecked at Egg Harbor with the loss of over 100 lives.

In 1999, the restored lighthouse tower opened to visitors. Since the renovation, visitors and staff claim dozens of inexplicable incidents. The unexplainable scent of pipe tobacco and cigar smoke wafts throughout the premises; disembodied footsteps resound in the tower and doors open and close on their own. Partial apparitions materialize, particularly an aged human hand appearing at the top of the lighthouse stairs. Dimes show up in odd locations, a classic spirit apport. (Apports are "gifts" manifested from the non-physical/spirit world to our physical realm.)

The Atlantic Paranormal Society, also known as TAPS, from Syfy Channel's *Ghost Hunters* TV series, conducted an investigation to assess the ghostly claims and haunting activity.

The professional ghost hunters heard an indecipherable conversation and the sound of footsteps. As they ascended the staircase, they realized the wind caused the noises. However, video evidence showed that a camera placed in the lighthouse mysteriously moved on its own and an odd light shone in the room!

Even though the *Ghost Hunters* unearthed minimal evidence during their visit, the accumulated first-hand experiences override the investigators initial findings. Take a gamble and check out this notoriously haunted spot.

Clara Barton Schoolhouse

100 Crosswicks Street
Bordentown

Born in North Oxford, Massachusetts, Clara Barton (1821–1912) taught school in her hometown as a young woman. In 1851, she visited friends in Hightstown and ended up teaching in the Cedar Swamp School. At the time few free public schools existed in New Jersey and Clara sought to encourage their development throughout the state. One year later she received the Bordentown school committee's approval to open a free public school and teach there. Under Clara's guidance, classroom attendance grew from six to 600 pupils the first year.

Clara's success impelled the town to build a new brick schoolhouse to better serve the students. When the new school opened in 1853, the town hired a male educator, and non-resident, to serve as principal instead of Barton. Adding insult to injury, they doubled his salary. A disheartened Barton left teaching in 1854 and moved to Washington, D.C. She later worked as a battlefield nurse in the Civil War and provided relief efforts during the Franco-Prussian War. She went on to found the American Red Cross in 1881 making the organization her life work.

In 1921, New Jersey students raised money to restore the tiny Bordentown schoolhouse in Barton's honor.

Patti DeSantis serves as President of the Bordentown Historical Society. She experienced inexplicable occurrences at the schoolhouse which sits across from her own home. Her first encounter happened inside the building during renovations. Removal of a ceiling panel exposed the attic opening where DeSantis noticed movement. For a brief moment, she observed a young boy's face while another boy stood behind him.

Another time as she set to work cleaning the classroom, DeSantis perceived a shadowy form appearing in each window as if somebody kept running around the building. She tried to chase down the culprit by running outside herself but the search revealed no one present. The spirits act like playful students but perhaps a trace of Clara's energy remains at her namesake school.

Emlen Physick Estate

1048 Washington Street
Cape May

The oldest seaside resort in the United States is New Jersey's most haunted city. Cape May is a designated national historic landmark and a museum of Victorian architecture. Over six hundred 19th century wooden structures ornament an area of less than two square miles.

Whalers first settled the region in the early 1600s. Two centuries later, steamship travel and rail service helped shape the town into a fashionable destination. Once known as the "playground of presidents," Abraham Lincoln lodged at the Mansion House in 1849, Franklin Pierce visited in 1855, James Buchanan vacationed here in 1858, Ulysses S. Grant in 1873 and Chester A. Arthur stayed in 1893.

Today, thousands of tourists crowd the tangled streets every year, sharing their space with illusions of earlier days. Phantom figures stroll along Congress Street, fishermen and visitors encounter eerie spirits along the coast and at the lighthouse. On Jackson Street, where the devastating 1836 fire consumed dozens of dwellings, denizens arrive at dawn and appear to be looking for their loved ones displaced during the fiery confusion.

The Mid-Atlantic Center for the Arts (MAC) is headquartered in a truly haunted mansion. The historically minded group saved the old manse from demolition in the 1970s. Built in 1879 for Dr. Emlen Physick, eccentric Philadelphia architect Frank Furness designed the stick-style, 18-room showplace. Physick's mother, Frances Ralsten and his aunts, Isabella and Emilie Parmentier, also resided with the good doctor.

The hauntings date to the mid-1940s when frightened residents quaked at living in the house because of its ghostly inhabitants. The family heard footsteps and noises every night and eventually gave up searching for the cause because it proved futile.

Psychic medium Craig McManus wrote three books concerning Cape May's hauntings. He identified several Physick Estate ephemeral residents including the most active wraith, Aunt Emilie, who stays behind to watch over the house. Although the doctor's mother successfully crossed over, her spirit remains in the house as residual energy, especially in her bedroom according to McManus. Another resident he identified is Isabelle, or Bella, Mrs. Ralston's invalid younger sister, who died in 1883, shortly after the family moved into the mansion.

The Carriage House is spirited by a servant, possibly a groomsman or driver. Several MAC staffers, whose offices are on the building's second floor, heard the wraith of the resident servant. Once his specter appeared in the dead of winter walking up to the entrance and into the building wrote McManus in *Ghosts of Cape May*.

MAC runs various ghost tours in the house year-round and attendees often encounter aspects of the paranormal first-hand. A visit to the Emlen Physick House could be an opportunity to experience your own ghost adventure.

Historic Cold Spring Village

720 U.S. Route 9
Cape May

Historic Cold Spring Village is a living history museum portraying daily life of a rural South Jersey community. From late June to early September, interpreters and artisans, wearing Early American period clothing, preserve the trades, crafts and heritage of a simpler time by demonstrating basket weaving, woodworking, blacksmithing, pottery making and other skills.

In addition to experiencing the village's 26 restored, historic buildings dating from 1691–1912, workshops and demonstrations are offered. The enclave is the perfect venue for programs highlighting spiritualism and the supernatural because for decades, village workers and visitors experienced the paranormal on-site.

The relocated buildings in the enclave, constructed over a period of two centuries, can exude an unearthly energy. At times an almost eerie ambiance pervades the little community. Occasionally the atmosphere feels thick with spirits from the past, says long-time village caretaker, Phil Calfina. Sometimes he witnesses three shawl-wrapped spectral women emerge from the Dennisville Inn. Originally located on Main Street in Dennisville, the 1836 Federal style building operated as a tavern on the Philadelphia to Cape May stage route. Back in the day taverns served as centers for town meetings and social gatherings as well as lodging places for travelers. In 1870, a Baptist owner acquired the property where he conducted church assemblies and meetings. The building features two front doors—one opens into the center hall and the other into the bar room. It seems the three female apparitions survive as leftover energy from the Baptist era yet they exit from the tavern door. 19th century custom prohibited women in bars so now that these ladies inhabit the afterlife perhaps they feel free to imbibe.

Calfina stated spirits exist all over the village. "I see them everywhere," he said. Calfina is not the only clairvoyant employee. Other staff members affirm the village is home to numerous spirits.

The charming Greek revival style Ewing-Douglass House accommodates the Ice Cream Parlor. Most likely farmer David Ewing built the house around 1850. In 1869, Nathaniel Douglass acquired the property and ran a country store in a side addition since removed. The spectral occupant is a petite woman who holds a lit candle as if standing vigil for a loved one.

Tammy Patterson interprets a 19th century housewife by demonstrating open-hearth cooking and gardening. While tending to her duties Tammy experienced a fright in the Spicer Leaming House. Built around 1820 on land now submerged under the Cape May Canal, the farmhouse belonged to the 17th century settler, Colonel Jacob Spicer and his Leaming descendants. In 1750, his son Jacob Spicer Esq. along with Aaron Leaming, published the "Concessions & Agreements," establishing freedom of religion, freedom of speech, trial by jury, elections and other rights for New Jersey citizens. Oddly, the ghost in residence is not related to the house's history.

Patterson said as she returned to the house after fetching water one day, she noticed a young girl staring out a second-story window. Patterson thought the girl was her new apprentice. She smiled and the girl smiled back. Patterson entered the home and went to welcome the girl but found no one there. Patterson's fright nearly caused her to quit her job. Although Patterson only sighted the apparition one time, the girl's ghost remains. The interpreter feels the phantom tug on her clothes, observes doors open and close on their own and watches the rocking chair move as if occupied. Patterson claims the young spirit seems to linger upstairs by a doll bed.

Smithville Mansion

803 Smithville Road
Eastampton Township

The Honorable Hezekiah B. Smith served as a congressman, inventor and leader of South Jersey's industrial revolution. He was also a bigamist. His life story reads like a blockbuster novel encompassing political intrigue, marital scandal, outrageous fortune, spurned love and haunting activity.

Born in 1816, the Honorable Mr. Smith served in Congress for one term and amassed a $500,000 fortune from the H.B. Smith Machine Factory he established. He held 40 patents for a steam powered tricycle, unique sewing machine and other designs. During his lifetime, the village where he founded his factory was renamed "Smithville" in his honor.

Smith also had two wives. He left his first wife, Eveline, and their four children, in Vermont to establish his New Jersey factory. Smith fell in love with Agnes Gilkerson; 23 years his junior, she attended the University of Pennsylvania. When Eveline refused a divorce, Smith burned all their correspondence, deleted his name from her family's Bible and disinherited their children. He

started his new life with Agnes disregarding his first marriage. Smithville residents were none the wiser. They knew Agnes as the one and only Mrs. Smith.

Agnes died at the young age of 43. Smith died six years later in 1887 and requested entombment in iron and concrete, clearly paranoid someone would steal his body. His son Elton did try. He sought to bring his father's body back to Vermont to lie beside his lawful wife as if to right his father's wrongs. When the crew tried to exhume Smith's body they struck the concrete and gave up.

In 1891, townspeople sighted Hezekiah Smith's ghost roaming the factory and mansion. The iron and concrete could not contain Smith's spirit. One townsman who spotted Smith's phantom a "dozen times" moved to Mount Holly due to fright, according to the *Washington Evening Star*. The newspaper also reported a story concerning a night watchman who "lost his reason" after repeated post-mortem visits by Smith's specter:

> *Several times as he [the night watchman] sat in the mill office the door would open and the ghostly form of Mr. Smith would enter, walk to the desk with his hands behind him in his usual way and after standing there for a while as if in thought he would slowly walk out toward the mansion. The constant repetition of these visits had such a terrifying effect on Gilbert's mind that he*

lost his reason and was today conveyed to
the asylum for the insane at Trenton.

Larry Gladfelter is the President of the Friends of the Mansion at Smithville (FOMAS). His connection to Smithville dates to 1981 and he's acquainted with some Smith descendants. Smith's full-bodied apparition appeared to Gladfelter several times sitting next to the pipe organ. Gladfelter theorizes Smith's presence remains because it is his home. FOMAS Trustee, Bill Stepler, experienced some odd incidents in the mansion like objects disappearing and strange smells. He said when Gladfelter plays the pipe organ there's a sudden drop in temperature.

Agnes and Elton's spirits may still haunt the house as well. The South Jersey Ghost Research group obtained eerie evidence. The investigators captured ghostly orbs on film and the group recorded a female voice saying, "Inside, come inside." Could this be Agnes' voice? On another recording a soft, clear voice whispers, "Watch out."

Union County Courthouse

2 Broad Street
Elizabeth

E arly settlers constructed a meeting house in 1668 at the corner of today's Broad Street and Rahway Avenue. The present day courthouse is the fourth government building to exist on the site. The court stands adjacent to the historic First Presbyterian Church, the resting place of Hannah Caldwell and her husband James, known as the "Fighting Parson."

When alerted to the enemy's approach on June 7, 1780, many fled Elizabethtown, but Hannah stood her ground trusting in Providence for protection. When British and Hessian soldiers entered the village, she retreated to a bedroom. An angry redcoat seeking revenge for the earlier defeat at nearby Connecticut Farms, jumped the fence into the Caldwell's yard. When Hannah, baby in her arms, looked out the window, the soldier discharged his musket. Two shots tore through her body and she fell lifeless to the floor, in the midst of her children.

When Reverend Caldwell arrived home the next day he found the village in ruins and his wife no more.

Hannah Caldwell's cold-blooded murder, as well as the wanton destruction of the peaceful hamlet, fueled resentment and converted Tories to Whigs. Hannah's death became a call to arms for mercenaries who assembled in unprecedented numbers to oppose the enemy.

Hannah's life and death inspired the design of the Union County Seal which is dedicated to the fallen patriot. Her enduring spirit is felt to this day. Some night workers allege Hannah's spirit cannot rest. Her diaphanous figure, dressed in white colonial clothing, floats down halls, through the parking garage and the church graveyard.

Other mysterious phenomena plague the courthouse. One maintenance worker avoids the elevator to the 14th floor because he perceives a strong sensation of paranoia. Sometimes when all is quiet, the elevator doors open. Heavy doors slam without benefit of human hand and bells ring in the rotunda. All the spooky incidents are attributed to Hannah's ghost. However, she may not be the culprit.

In the 19th century, executions by hanging took place outside the courthouse. All offenders were convicted of murder. Some feel the spirits of those hanged behind the building are to blame for the inexplicable incidents.

Syfy Channel's *Ghost Hunters* searched for spirits in the courthouse in 2009. In reviewing the evidence, a female apparition in the Records Room appeared on the video. Even more astonishing is the apparition appears to walk through the wall! Is this Hannah's legendary ghost? The fact is the paranormal activity within the Union County Courthouse is legit.

Historic Village at Allaire

4263 Atlantic Avenue
Farmingdale

In 1822, James Allaire purchased the Howell Works as a resource for his New York City based Allaire Iron Works. At the time, his company led the manufacture of marine steam engines. He cast the brass air chamber for Robert Fulton's *Clermont* and sailed with Fulton on the steamboat's historic maiden voyage. The Howell Works also manufactured cast iron products. Allaire eventually transformed the site into a self-sufficient community, complete with housing and food supply for the workforce and its own post office, church, school and company store. The town even issued its own currency.

Bog iron production became obsolete by the increasing availability of iron ore. In 1846, the Howell Works furnace was outmoded. Allaire continued living in his village, while maintaining his New York business, until his death in 1858. When he died, the town's name changed to Allaire, New Jersey.

Today's Historic Village at Allaire is a notable example of an early American company town. The settlement is also noteworthy for its ghostly inhabitants. In the

Visitors Center for instance, psychics detect a strong, male energy. The entity is described as a nasty, angry man who wears boots. History records Benjamin Marks as the village supervisor who lived in one of the early row houses rebuilt on the original foundation. Marks disliked his job according to clairsentients who "read" his energy. One morning as staffers performed their routine security check in the cellar they heard heavy footfalls. They cautiously approached the interloper and confronted the partial apparition of a man in boots! They suspect this encounter is a postmortem visit from the tyrannical manager. Other mystifying manifestations include electrical anomalies—lights, projectors, cameras and security systems usually go haywire without cause.

Eric Mabius is an actor whose father became the museum director at Historic Allaire Village in the 1980s. The Mabius family lived on site and Eric and his brother considered the 330-acre park their playground. One foggy night they approached the "Big House," the founder's former residence. Dim security lights illumined the empty house as Mabius peered through the window in response to inconsolable sobbing he heard coming from inside. He observed a tall figure dressed in funeral garb including a top hat. The man didn't seem "right," Mabius said. The apparition seemed inconsolable and turned his head toward Mabius and looked him straight in the eye. The sighting terrified the actor and troubled him for years.

The "Happy Medium," Kim Russo, hosts the LMN documentary television series *The Haunting Of...* In 2012, Eric Mabius appeared on the program in an effort to obtain an explanation for his disturbing experience.

When a cholera epidemic hit New York City in 1832, James Allaire moved his family to the Howell village but to no avail. His wife, Frances, perished from the disease.

Russo's vision of a woman languishing in an upstairs bedroom validated the sad event.

Frances' death triggered a downward spiral for Allaire. Shortly thereafter, a ship he jointly owned, the

William Gibbons, ran aground and wrecked. The same year, the Howell Works furnace blew and production temporarily ceased. The following year, America plunged into a severe recession and Allaire's uninsured steamboat *Home*, sank with the loss of 100 lives. The catastrophe damaged Allaire's reputation and practically wiped him out financially.

Another ghost in residence is Hal Allaire. He also haunts the Big House and his playful spirit enjoys taunting the costumed interpreters who work in the building. Hal lived at Allaire as a virtual recluse until his death in 1901. Without the funds to maintain the site the buildings fell into disrepair. The property became known as the Deserted Village of Allaire. The otherworldly Hal is a mischievous poltergeist who likes to move books and household objects. He apparently possesses a fondness for playing with candles as well. This proclivity became evident when Russo, who discerned Hal's presence along with his father's, posed questions to the men. The lighted candle on the table responded quite animatedly during the show.

The Historic Village at Allaire is an epicenter of ghostly activity. The village offers a spooky hayride, a haunted mansion, ghost stories, paranormal experts and tarot card readings around Halloween. All events are family friendly and not scary—unless you look in the windows of the Big House...

Old Schoolhouse Museum

126 U.S. Route 9
Forked River

The Lacey Historical Society preserves artifacts and lore of the local region in the Old Schoolhouse Museum. The 1868 school remained in use until 1952 when a new grade school opened. Ten years later, the historical society headquartered in the old building where displays of tools, utensils, furniture and other mementoes of daily life are exhibited.

Elizabeth McGrath is the vice-president of the historical society and she says something spooky happens every time she's alone in the museum. For instance, she finds photos moved from one place to another and doll carriages also change position. The phone will ring yet there is no one on the line. The printer fails for no reason but later operates perfectly. The glass bookcase, where photos of barefoot pupils are displayed, is found open. Elizabeth believes the presence is the leftover energy of one or more former students.

These days, paranormal investigators assist in validating supernatural experiences. The historical society called in the Southern Jersey Shore Paranormal Research team to evaluate the eerie situation. Elizabeth and several other museum members assisted the paranormal group headed by Lori Flurchick. It literally was a dark and stormy night when the ghost hunters arrived with their equipment on a Friday the 13th.

Operating in the dark, team members used tape recorders, motion detectors and video cameras to determine the presence of unusual energies. In one room the temperature dropped seven degrees within minutes. The chandelier crystals swayed back and forth as if manipulated by unseen hands. Elizabeth actually flaunted goose bumps as the team called out to a presence they sensed in the museum. Despite brand new batteries installed in their equipment, some of their apparatus failed. The team succeeded in recording over a dozen responses to questions posed to the spirits including uncanny children's voices.

Gabreil Daveis Tavern

Fourth Avenue
Glendora

*"On the floor are mysterious footsteps,
There are whispers along the walls!"*
—HENRY WADSWORTH LONGFELLOW

The Georgian style, 1756 colonial tavern is one of New Jersey's oldest historical landmarks. In earlier days, the Gloucester County tavern served as an inn for boatmen who transported their products to Philadelphia via Big Timber Creek. Taverns, or "ordinaries" as they were also called, were essential during the colonial era. Transportation modes of the day required a hostelry every few miles on main thoroughfares so weary and hungry travelers could find refreshment. Taverns became public meeting places in early America. People congregated in the roadhouses to hear travelers' tales, the latest news and sometimes heated political arguments ensued fueled by spirits of the alcoholic kind.

George Washington designated the stone building as a field hospital during the American Revolution. The third floor lodged the most grievously wounded.

Soldiers rested, recovered and died there. Some remain in a perpetual state of unrest. Although their names are forgotten, their post-mortem presence fills the garret with a sickening feeling and their blood still stains the floorboards. Some clairaudients detect the sounds of tormented men suffering the wounds of war. Several photos taken in the house reveal light orbs. Especially prevalent in the attic, paranormal researchers contend the presence of orbs indicates a ghostly expression.

To add to the spookiness, specters sighted in the woods out back turn and flee as if they're encroaching on inhospitable turf. Some assert these skulking shades are former spies.

Greenfield Hall

343 Kings Highway East
Haddonfield

Greenfield Hall serves as headquarters for the Historical Society of Haddonfield. The structure is the third home built on the property. John Gill IV built the red brick, Georgian-style home incorporating two small rooms on the east side—remnants of the 1747 John Gill II house. John Gill IV owned and farmed large tracts of land in Haddonfield and participated in banking and politics. The house retains its original 1841 appearance and its rooms are furnished in keeping with the period. The building is more than a house museum and other rooms display various items relating to Haddonfield's history. Antique New Jersey glass, needlework samplers and 18th century costumes; a pottery exhibit, doll and toy collection along with a tool museum add appeal. One playful spirit seems overly fond of the tools and other objects. Oftentimes items disappear and later reappear somewhere else in the house.

Count Carl Emil Ulrich von Donop was a Hessian colonel who fought in the American Revolutionary War. British General William Howe assigned Fort Mercer's capture to von Donop. When Von Donop requested additional artillery, Howe replied that if von Donop could not take the fort, the British would. The Hessian's angry response read, "Either that will be Fort Donop or I shall be dead."

On the evening of October 21, 1777, Colonel von Donop and his troops arrived in Haddonfield. As the soldiers bivouacked in the fields beyond the village, Colonel von Donop selected John Gill's house as his headquarters. Families who entertained officers were secure against pillage, so many inhabitants opened their doors. Even though John Gill was a staunch Quaker, and therefore a pacifist, von Donop's refinement won him over.

After the Hessians departed, John Gill informed his relative Ann Whitall, (see Whitall House, National Park), that the Hessians were coming—thanks to von Donop broadcasting his plan to capture Fort Mercer the night before.

Now at Fort Mercer, von Donop summoned Colonel Christopher Greene to surrender. He declined. Von Donop's 2,000 men attacked the 400 member continental army. Brandishing his sword, von Donop headed the charge. Struck by a musket ball in the hip, he fell mortally wounded and died three days later. The Count was buried on the battlefield but he would not rest in peace.

Looters desecrated von Donop's grave according to author William E. Meehan, Jr. Meehan conducts ghost tours in Haddonfield. He writes in *Haunted Haddonfield* that grave robbers stole von Donop's uniform, bones and even his gravestone; a physician took his skull. Meehan goes on to say, *"On the anniversaries of the eve of the battle, lights in the second floor room of the 1747 east wing [of the Gill House] have lit by themselves."* Might von Donop be burning the midnight oil to thank the Gill's for his last pleasant evening on earth or does he still plot to take over the patriot fort?

Batsto Mansion

31 Batsto Road
Hammonton

The Batsto Village Restoration and nearby Atsion Lake located in Wharton State Forest offer a glimpse of life in the Pine Barrens from the 1760s to the 1850s.

In 1766, Charles Read built the Batsto Iron Works along the Batsto River. The area offered the natural resources necessary for making iron—bog ore was extracted from the banks of streams and rivers, trees fueled the fire and water powered the manufacturing process. The iron works produced household wares such as cooking pots and kettles. During the Revolutionary War, Batsto manufactured supplies for the continental army.

In 1784, William Richards managed the industry and erected a 32-room mansion for his family and generations of future ironmasters.

By the mid-1800s, iron production declined and Batsto became a glassmaking community known for the production of windowpanes. Joseph Wharton, a Philadelphia businessman, purchased Batsto in 1876. Wharton continued to increase his property holdings in the surrounding area and improved many village buildings. His renovation of the ironmaster's mansion transformed the structure into the elegant Italianate manse we know today. The impressive structure is the village's centerpiece and reflects the prosperity enjoyed during Batsto's heyday. Fourteen rooms, including the parlors, dining room, library and bedrooms are open to the public.

Some visitors claim the place is haunted according to Charles Adams III who wrote *Ghosts of Atlantic County*. He says certain sightseers observe a figure peering out the upper story windows. A few even captured a human likeness in their photos. At night, when the mansion is vacant, some allege to see lights on the third floor. A few individuals said they felt a persistent, disembodied tap on their shoulder.

During the 1930s and 40s, Elizabeth Brown Pezzuto's aunt and uncle served as caretakers at the mansion. Elizabeth recalls her uncle ascending the winding staircase at night with an oil lamp to light his way. The lantern cast eerie, flickering shadows which gave her goose bumps. Perhaps the pranks played by Elizabeth and her sisters precipitated the mansion's haunted reputation. When the girls would hear visitors approaching the house to peek in the windows, as sightseers do today, the sisters grabbed sofa pillows and hid under the windowsills. As they listened to people's comments gazing through the windowpanes, the girls remained out of sight and tossed the pillows in the air to give the peeping toms a good scare.

Although today's technology helps to confirm the existence of ghosts, proof is elusive at the Wharton Mansion and remains up in the air.

Hancock House

3 Front Street
Hancock's Bridge

Judge William Hancock's house is an excellent example of Flemish masonry, distinctive brickwork unique to southwest New Jersey. The 1734 structure boasts a brick herringbone design on its end walls and a checkerboard brick pattern on the front and back. During the Revolutionary War, a brutal massacre occurred at the site.

Hancock, who despite his American sympathies, served as an official in the British colonial government. He functioned as a justice of the peace loyal to King George III.

In March 1778, while the local militia quartered at Hancock's residence, Tories, under the command of Major John Graves Simcoe, foraged the area for food and supplies. (John Simcoe is a central villain in the AMC TV drama *Turn, Washington's Spies*). Simcoe crossed Alloway Creek and raided Judge Hancock's house, killing 30 American rebels in their sleep and wounding five others. William Hancock was also killed.

Within a week of the massacre, the British contingent left Salem County behind. The blood staining the attic floor is an eerie relic of their awful slaughter. For some soldiers the gory residue is not enough to keep their memory alive. Patriot spirits linger here patrolling the Hancock House; their screams and moans some- times emanates in the building. Clairvoyants say the soldiers continue to re-enact the car- nage in another dimension.

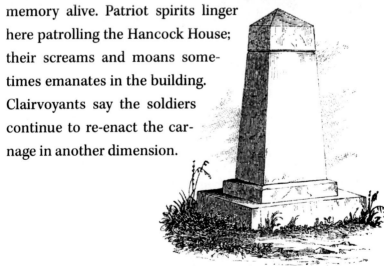

The Hermitage

335 North Franklin Turnpike
Ho-Ho-Kus

I n 1767, Ann Bartow DeVisme moved to Ho-Ho-Kus
from Manhattan with five children. She purchased
The Hermitage, a two-story, Dutch-inspired brownstone
built in 1763. One of Ann's daughters, Theodosia Bartow
Prevost, and her husband James Marcus Prevost, occupied
another house on the property. During the American
Revolution, while Loyalist Major Prevost fought for the
British in the South, the women and children were left
alone in Ho-Ho-Kus.

In July 1778, George Washington and his troops, flush with victory over the successful campaign at Monmouth Courthouse, passed through Ho-Ho-Kus on their way to White Plains, New York. When the General and his entourage stopped at a local house, Theodosia sent an invitation to Washington to come and stay at The Hermitage. Homes that welcomed military officers were secure against pillage. The U.S. troops were entertained at The Hermitage for four days, July 10–14, 1778. During the visit, Theodosia met Aaron Burr.

After her husband was killed in the war, Theodosia married Burr at The Hermitage on July 2, 1782. She met many of the attending guests during the numerous times she opened her house to soldiers. Guests of the wedding included Lord Stirling, James Monroe, the Marquis de Lafayette, Peggy Shippen Arnold and Alexander Hamilton.

The house passed through three subsequent owners before it was sold in 1807 to local physician Elijah Rosencrantz and his wife, Cornelia. In 1847, Elijah II commissioned an architect to design a romantic Victorian residence incorporating the historic Hermitage. The result is the Gothic Revival style structure with gable roofs and diamond-paned windows existing today as a National Historic Landmark and house museum.

The couple's daughter, Mary Elizabeth, was born on-site in 1885 and lived there for 85 years until her death in 1970. Her faithful companion and former servant, Katie Zahner, died five days later. Unmarried and one of the last Rosencrantz descendants, Mary Elizabeth realized the home's historical value. She willed the property to the State of New Jersey for use as a museum and park.

To preserve the historic property for posterity, Mary Elizabeth and Katie endured years of hardship. Due to high heating costs, they resided in only two rooms relying on a woodstove for warmth and cooking. The Red Cross brought the pair food and they received gifts of coal from railroad workers. The women even defended the property from trespassers and vandals. When Mary Elizabeth and Katie fell ill in 1969, social service installed electricity in one room. Mary Elizabeth routinely refused offers to purchase the five-acre manor even though selling meant comfort for the aging women; she remained steadfast in her fight to save the historically significant property.

A long-held Hermitage mystery promulgated by Mary Elizabeth and perpetuated down through the years is the "secret room." The unremarkable storage space turned spectacular in tantalizing stories recounted by Mary Elizabeth and her Aunt Bess to promote their popular Tea Room in the 1920s. One tale told of a human skeleton dressed in a disintegrating Hessian uniform discovered in the small space.

The Hermitage's role in our nation's history is noteworthy and the spirits who haunt the property add further appeal.

In the 1970s, as officials conferred on-site whether to repair the cedar barn or demolish the building, an African

American woman in a long skirt walked out of the barn. The woman, who carried a baby in her arms, passed in front of them. One of the bureaucrats asked what she was doing there. The woman didn't respond... she simply vanished. Locals believe the specter is one of two slaves who lived at the property in 1860, their names Gin and Sylva.

After Mary Elizabeth passed away, the Hermitage fell into disrepair. The grounds grew dark and ominous and the house decayed. Those who dared to trespass sometimes heard piano music emanating from inside the forsaken structure. Some locals who passed by the house often claimed to see a light inside. Barely discernible, the flickering glow traveled from room to room as if Mary Elizabeth's indomitable spirit performed a post-mortem vigil, roaming the manse with a candle to watch over the space.

The museum's curator said staffers sometimes share stories of hearing a woman wailing, ephemeral piano music, lights turning off and on and feelings of an unseen presence. Some even sense the touch of an invisible hand and sometimes the scent of perfume permeates the place. At a recent séance, a metronome set on the old piano stared to move on its own. Perhaps Mary Elizabeth is letting us know her devotion to her home has not skipped a beat.

> *"We meet them at the doorway, on the stair,*
> *Along the passages they come and go,*
> *Impalpable impressions on the air,*
> *A sense of something moving to and fro."*
> —HENRY WADSWORTH LONGFELLOW

River Road School

400 Riverside Avenue
Lyndhurst

In 1804, Jacob Van Winkle donated property for the construction of a school. The annual rental charge was one peppercorn, "if demanded." County officials erected a one-room schoolhouse and in 1893, the River Road School went up. The structure served as an active school into the

1980s. The Lyndhurst Historical Society eventually leased the historic relic to preserve the landmark building.

Commonly known as the "Little Red Schoolhouse," the school museum focuses on local history and features a circa 1912 classroom complete with artifacts, memorabilia and some say a ghost.

In the past, some observed the apparition of a woman dressed in an antique white blouse and a long, beige skirt. At times the teacher's specter materialized as a full-bodied apparition while at other times she appeared transparent. When the light-haired phantom revealed herself, she seemed to be lost in her own world as she gathered firewood in her arms. Her movements mimicked the placement of invisible logs in the pot-bellied stove and the lighting of a fire.

Mead Hall

36 Madison Avenue
Madison

Who is haunting Mead Hall at Drew University? Most feel it's the spirit of Roxanna Mead Drew.

The former wife of Wall Street banker and Drew Theological Seminary founder Daniel Drew, died in 1876 but some feel her spirit never left this mortal coil.

Students hear footsteps on the main staircase and elsewhere in the building as do some maintenance workers and security personnel, all of whom work the night shift. Security guards routinely report doors bang shut on their own and one night an inner office door slammed behind them with an unexplainable force.

In 1833, Savannah plantation owner, William Gibbons built the Greek-revival style manse as a northern home for his growing family and ever expanding stable of thoroughbred race horses. Financier Daniel Drew purchased the estate in 1867 to establish Drew Theological Seminary. He christened the mansion Mead Hall, in honor of his wife, Roxanna Mead.

A horrific fire occurred in the building on August 24, 1989 and burned for 23 hours despite the efforts of 16 surrounding fire companies. During the blaze, Madison firefighters spotted a woman walking unfazed through the raging flames. They moved toward her, calling out to lead her to safety. They suddenly realized her old-fashioned attire seemed out of place and a second later, she vanished before their eyes. Supposedly a photographer captured the image of a female in the middle of the blaze and the photo bears a striking resemblance to Roxanna.

A painting of Roxanna, hangs in Mead Hall's lobby. Some students feel the portrait emits a haunting aura and perceived the feeling of being followed when walking past the image. It's said Roxanna's ghost continues to walk the hallowed halls.

Burrowes Mansion

94 Main Street
Matawan

Built in 1723, the Burrowes Mansion became the home of grain merchant John Burrowes Sr. and his son Major John Burrowes Jr. At the time of the Revolution, Burrowes Sr. assumed the nickname "Corn King" as he traded mainly in grain. The Patriot Burrowes clan stood as proud members of the Sons of Liberty. After the Boston Tea Party, he actively supported the Boston patriots with food and money. When the first New Jersey militia formed they mustered in Burrowes' front yard.

John Burrowes Jr. served as a Major during the war. His wife, Margaret, continued to live in the house to hold the fort, so to speak. The Major returned to visit the homestead when on furlough. Local Tories targeted Burrowes for capture and actively scouted the house. During one of his stays on May 27, 1778, they raided the Burrowes property to seize the Major. He escaped their clutches but his father, John Sr., did not fare as well. The invaders set several outbuildings, including mills and storehouses, ablaze but spared the house.

Throughout the attack, Margaret Burrowes brazenly stood her ground on the home's grand staircase. She boldly refused the demand of a British soldier to hand over her shawl to staunch an officer's bloody wound. In retaliation, the soldier stabbed Margaret through the chest with his bayonet. It's alleged Margaret's steadfast specter still stands her ground on the stairway and refuses to give up the ghost.

Margaret isn't the only wraith in residence. Docents hear disembodied footsteps and indistinguishable voices. In general, auditory apparitions are the most common event among supernatural experiences. As the Burrowes Mansion historian informed Patrick Kurdes and his Paranormal Activity Research Society (PARS) team about two young girls who haunt the living room, they heard movement on the second floor and a young girl giggle. During the group's investigation, researcher Marina invited any resident spirits to touch her hair. Subsequently, Marina screamed and jumped off her chair when she felt someone stroke her tresses.

Various other ghost hunters captured several instances of electronic voice phenomenon (EVP); recorded voices of the dead are imperceptible until played back on taping devices. Whispered declarations like, "Be gone," "Are you the Corn King?" or "Your son is dead" are examples of the EVPs recorded, according to Matawan Historical Society trustee Al Savolaine. Another recorded spirit voice in the attic said "help." The attic once served as the servants' quarters and it's where PARS photographed a ghost in the window.

The museum faithfully depicts an earlier time familiar to the spirits who once enjoyed the comfortable space. The site is gently spirited by a poltergeist who likes to move items from place to place. Could this be Margaret's spirit placing objects where she thinks they ought to be?

A distant Burrowes relative, who at first didn't realize the house's mystic reputation, captured a light anomaly in one of the windows when she snapped a photograph. Margaret Burrowes' spectral image, she presumed, and she's probably right.

Thomas Budd House

20 White Street
Mount Holly

In the early 1720s, a dam constructed on Rancocas Creek channeled water through a mill race to power grist and saw mills. After the mills were established, the area attracted more settlers who built houses and commercial buildings on the surrounding streets. Today the raceway is mill free but the channel follows its original course from Rancocas Creek.

Mill Race Village is part of a restored historic neighborhood and a haven for entrepreneurs, artisans and professionals. The historic Budd House is centered among many haunted buildings in the village. One theory suggests a correlation between running water and paranormal activity. Running water generates electric current and spirits may "feed" off the electrical charge enabling them to manifest.

The 1744 Thomas Budd House is the third earliest known residence on its original site in Mount Holly. Budd worked as a cooper out of his brick home, making barrels to hold the flour from the grist mill. He lived in the house with his wife for only seven years, dying of unknown causes in 1751. Throughout its history, the house served

as a stop on the Underground Railroad. A tunnel enabling escape still exists in the basement. At one time, the structure also functioned as a museum but now serves as private residences with retail space on the lower floor.

The house is the site of a Hessian soldier's murder. Enraged locals stabbed and killed him with a bayonet because he assaulted a young girl. Others claim he was a traitor killed by his comrades. Regardless, his smelly spirit stays behind manifesting as an angry presence stomping about in heavy boots. Originally held captive in the basement, his tall, shadowy figure roams all over the building frightening more than 20 individuals.

Clairvoyants identify the most dominant presence as an early 19th century caretaker. They describe him having long, straggly, gray hair, blue eyes and bad teeth. His residual movements mimicked lamp lighting and the carrying of a ring of keys. According to psychics, the steward prefers the stillness of the basement—-he abhors all the activity upstairs. A melancholy female spirit lingers in the cellar as well; her sadness palpable to clairsentients.

The ghostly population includes spectral men wearing tri-cornered hats, an 18th century woman wearing a full-length blue dress and a little boy phantom. When South Jersey Ghost Research investigated the building, some members experienced light-headedness and nausea, as do some merchants and shoppers. They claimed the little boy's spirit followed them around desperate for someone to play with.

Acorn Hall

68 Morris Avenue
Morristown

Dr, John Schermerhorn built Acorn Hall as a private residence in 1853. The Italianate-style structure boasts an unusual octagonal tower. Today the Morris County Historical Society operates the house museum, a virtual time-capsule decorated mainly with furnishings from the two families who lived there between 1853 and 1971. Acorn Hall authentically represents Morris County's upper-middle class suburban life.

Listed on both the New Jersey State and National Registers of Historic Places, the hall is part of the New Jersey Women's Heritage Trail. This placement recognizes the role of former owners, Crane and Hone who contributed to historic preservation and the women's suffrage movement. Acorn Hall's period garden connects to a trail that leads to the neighboring Frelinghuysen Arboretum.

The Victorian house is also the perfect setting for a ghost story, albeit a sad one. The specter in residence is Louise, the young widow of the home's first owner, Dr. John Schermerhorn. Tragically, Louise died in child birth at the age of 24. Schermerhorn only lived in the house five years after his wife's untimely death. The museum's recreation of an atmosphere familiar to the lingering Louise probably makes her feel right at home.

Astoundingly, Louise's full-bodied apparition descending the stairs is the most frequent paranormal phenomenon. Witnesses who observed the widow's ghost describe her wearing a taffeta dress and bonnet with a wicker basket on her arm. The distinct sounds of footsteps and a crinkling skirt accompany her appearance. Perhaps she is on her way outside to gather flowers from the authentic gardens.

Whitall House

100 Hessian Avenue
National Park

As the Battle of Red Bank raged along the Delaware River, Ann Whitall calmly worked on her spinning wheel according to legend. Quakers James and Ann Whitall, built their home on the Delaware River in 1748. For over one hundred years four generations inhabited the Georgian home. The house stood at the center of Whitall's 400-acre plantation amid orchards, livestock, grist mill, a ferry crossing, smoke house and shad fishery.

Colonel Christopher Greene, American force commander in Mercer, chose the Whitall House as his headquarters during the American Revolution. The

Colonel pronounced the family's apple orchard the ideal location for a defensive fort, so his men razed the grove and constructed Fort Mercer. The trenches dug along the fort's perimeter still exist.

Hessian soldiers still smarted from their embarrassing defeat at the Battle of Trenton in December, 1776. In retaliation, they sought to overthrow the Colonial forces at Fort Mercer. "Loose lips sink ships," as the saying goes... two drunken British soldiers let down their guard over pints in a local pub. A patriot sympathizer overhead their strategy and quickly informed the Colonials. As a result, on October 22, 1777, Count Emil von Donop and 2000 troops were soundly trounced by 400 American forces. Fatally wounded, von Donop died three days later. He was buried on Red Bank Battlefield along with the other casualties. Inadvertently, Whitall's former fruit orchard turned into a graveyard.

The Whitalls' home became a field hospital out of necessity. The embattled men lodged on every floor after the battle, including the attic, and many died there. Ann Whitall tended the wounded with healing herbs that she grew in her garden. The stench and torment of the suffering soldiers eventually overwhelmed the family. They left their home and returned in the spring to work the plantation.

Purchased by the United States government in 1872, the property is now a museum maintained by the Daughters of the American Revolution. Each year

thousands visit the 44-acre historical park which includes remnants of Fort Mercer, walking paths, pavilions, picnic groves, a pier and a playground.

Between 1872 and 1980, various caretakers occupied the site. Elaine Allen is the granddaughter of the house's last warden. She grew up on the property during the 1930s and '40s and said sometimes piano music echoed throughout the home even though no piano existed in the house. She also heard what sounded like someone reading a newspaper at the breakfast table. Locked doors unlocked and doors opened on their own. According to Ms. Allen, one day a black cat walked across the kitchen floor and vanished.

Curator Kathryn Dodson's research uncovered a family history detailing the house ghosts. In 1879, Hannah Whitall Smith, the great-great-granddaughter of James and Ann Whitall, wrote the ghost stories of wounded men haunting the attic frightened her as a child. Her uncle often awoke to violent rattling caused by the pitcher in the wash basin. Already filled with fear, when the door opened with great force he hid under the covers 'til daybreak.

Smith also noted the appearance of spectral uniformed officers (Count von Donop perhaps?) in the stairways and halls. These highly trafficked areas hold a lot of energy. Stairways and halls store energy and somehow replays events that we sense as paranormal phenomena. According to Smith, a visitor once observed the 18th century spirit of a "courtly looking Frenchman with a lady on his arm dressed in the quaint old costumes."

Genuine mystics can be a useful in interpreting paranormal phenomenon even though skeptics doubt the ability. A defensible viewpoint for sure, considering charlatans exist in every walk of life. When one psychic offers information then a number of others suggest similar scenarios, that's evidence. Individuals with extra sensory perception who visited the Whitall property detected wails, unintelligible voices and spectral soldiers. Park rangers also attest to hearing disembodied utterances.

The Perceptive Paranormal Research (PPR) team encountered haunting activity as well. While in the main hospital room, PPR investigator Amanda Staszak felt a touch on her elbow. She said the contact felt like someone took her arm to move her out of the way.

A visit to the Whitall House is a must and rest assured you will not be elbowed out of the way—but then again, maybe you will be.

Shippen Manor

8 Belvidere Avenue
Oxford

The Oxford Furnace is listed on the State and National Registers of Historic Places. Built in 1741, it was the third furnace in Colonial New Jersey and the first iron ore mining operation. Prior to that time, ore was scooped out of bogs in South Jersey.

The Shippens were a wealthy Philadelphia family. Joseph Shippen, Jr. acquired the Oxford Furnace site around 1741. William Shippen II built the manor circa 1765-70. The estate contained over four thousand acres including land on the Delaware River and a grant from the King of England to operate a ferry. The Manor is

Georgian in style, constructed from local stone, two foot thick stone walls and three immense chimneys.

Joseph W. Shippen managed the property beginning in 1760. Tenant farms surrounded the self-sufficient iron plantation which included various mills and a store as well as the iron furnace. Joseph employed Martha Axford, a local farm girl, as housekeeper. During her "housekeeping" tenure she bore him seven children. No record exists of a marriage.

A member of the Continental Congress, William Shippen II became a self-taught physician and treated George Washington, Benjamin Franklin, John Hancock, the Marquis de Lafayette and others.

The State of New Jersey purchased the property in 1974 and eventually the Shippen Manor Museum opened in 1995. Costumed docents lead tour groups, demonstrate open-hearth cooking and period musicians perform on occasion. Each summer the property hosts free outdoor concerts.

According to some staff members, unexplainable events occur from time to time. A Revolutionary War specter appears in the reception area where the door tends to open and close on its own. In the dining room, a little boy wearing old-fashioned clothing materialized to staff and visitors and a female spirit dressed in blue attire appeared in the Victorian Parlor. In the attic, one visitor experienced a forceful burst of air that blasted through them. Museum curators say Civil War artifacts not in the museum's inventory appear in a cupboard. Since many objects in the museum originated from outside donors the items could carry residual energies that trigger haunting activity.

The Syfy Channel's *Ghost Hunters* crew visited the manor four times. The Atlantic Paranormal Society (TAPS) experienced events similar to the haunted claims endured by the site's staff and visitors. TAPS members felt someone *whoosh* by them. An impression sensed by several staff members as well. They heard disembodied voices and observed items move on their own. Team leaders Grant Wilson and Jason Hawes spotted a person's shadow standing over a table—the same place where earlier witnesses saw the spectral soldier. The ghost hunters' equipment recorded footsteps as well as a child's voice.

During the client reveal, Jason played back the recording he captured when something *whooshed* by him. The noise sounded like somebody running. Another recording captured a small voice saying, "Uh-oh," after the sound of something fallen is heard. Grant declared the investigation a success and the manor house haunted with benevolent, intelligent spirits.

Proprietary House

149 Kearny Avenue
Perth Amboy

A plethora of spirits haunt Perth Amboy's Proprietary House, one of New Jersey's most haunted dwellings. Psychic Jane Doherty regularly conducts public séances in the royal mansion. Her sessions perturb the resident spirits some of which include a Revolutionary War solder, a woman in white and a little boy in blue. A deliveryman once claimed the little blue boy let him into the house and led him to the third floor.

The 1764 house was home to His Excellency William Franklin, the last royal Governor of the Province of New Jersey. In 1775, Benjamin Franklin, signer of the Declaration of Independence, journeyed to Perth Amboy to persuade his son to switch his allegiance. The senior statesman pleaded, ranted and raved, but William stood his ground. Benjamin grieved over his failure to convert William and later wrote to a friend, "I am deserted by my only son."

Governor Franklin was imprisoned in 1776 for supporting the British and exiled to England. He died a lonely, broken man. His spirit is very much alive at his former imperial manse, however, where his stormy specter stomps about lamenting all he lost.

President Emeritus of the Proprietary House Association, Donald J. Peck, knows all about the haunted happenings at the country's only remaining royal governor's mansion. Peck said heavy footsteps often resound inside the house. Incredibly, this writer heard the thud of purposeful strides overhead during a Jane Doherty séance. Could the pensive pacing be William's spirit mulling over his options?

After the Revolution, fire destroyed the interior of the house. Eventually the building was restored, enlarged and established as the Brighton House. For a few years, the hotel catered to the rich and fashionable, but business dwindled during the War of 1812.

The atmospheric wine cellar serves as a tearoom. Peck said a visitor once observed a spectral Revolutionary War soldier walk right *through* the brick wall. Oftentimes, invisible guests seem to enjoy an otherworldly tea break. Volunteers find two chairs pulled out from the table, as if occupied by patrons, and two cups righted on the saucers when normally the cups are set upside down.

Sometimes during a formal tea, the embarrassing stench of horse manure filters through from another realm. In the distant past, animals lodged in the house to protect them from marauding adversaries. The ladies room is another area where a mischievous spirit likes to detain occupants by locking the door. Locals assert the place remains haunted by the specter of a little boy dressed in blue antique garb. (Is he a revenant from the Brighton House?). Neighbors say they see him knocking at the front door and even claim he sometimes plays in their yards.

Some visitors also hear disembodied voices along with footsteps and feel unseen hands grasp at them. In the ballroom, spectral images appear in the old mirror. The Atlantic Paranormal Society (TAPS) investigated the house and featured their session on a *Ghost Hunters* episode. TAPS felt comfortable saying there is definitely paranormal activity going on.

Without question, old Perth Town's royal palace continues to intrigue historians and ghost hunters alike.

Metlar-Bodine House

1281 River Road
Piscataway

Originally settled in 1666, the Metlar-Bodine House is one of two original dwellings in Piscataway. Built in 1728 by merchant Peter Bodine, the one room home, with sleeping loft and root cellar, perched on a bluff overlooking the Raritan River. Expanded in the 1850s, the present 14-room Colonial mansion changed hands several times before entrepreneur George Metlar, a real estate magnate who owned thousands of acres in Piscataway, purchased the property in the 1890s.

Metlar and his next-door neighbor, John Field, engaged in a long-standing feud. No one knows what caused the dispute or when it started. Anecdotal evidence suggests Metlar's animosity continued into the afterlife. Visitors hear unexplained noises and feel cold spots whenever Field's name is mentioned. Once Field's photograph flew off the mantle and across the room. Was Metlar sending a message from the great beyond?

The historic house operates as a museum and presents state and local history. During renovations in 1993, the repairs revived the home's spectral revenants. Spirits can

be perturbed when their environment suddenly shifts; alterations may be confusing and/or they may not like the changes to their home.

So many witnesses reported apparitions and mysterious phenomena that the strange goings-on were ultimately featured on *The Today Show*. Museum members spotted a man sporting a black bowler hat walk down the corridor and vanish. A female dressed in a long gown lounged by the fireplace in the parlor. The caretaker heard someone humming ancient sea ballads in the attic. Sometimes passersby observed a bearded man waving from an upstairs window even though the building sat vacant.

Seabrook Wilson House

719 Port Monmouth Road
Port Monmouth

The Seabrook Wilson Homestead is the most haunted house in Monmouth County—possibly the nation. The structure started out as a one-room residence built by Thomas Whitlock in 1648. Initially known as Strawberry Hill, the Spy House nickname evolved during the Revolutionary War. Historians debate the building's function as a tavern during the era but most feel the house survived the Revolution by operating as an inn. As British mercenaries imbibed, the patriot innkeeper eavesdropped and passed along the enemies' secrets to the Colonials. This tactic resulted in the "Spy House" moniker.

The infamous "woman in white" is the most dramatic manifestation reported. Sighted on the second floor, the female apparition moves about and seems to straighten bedclothes. Always oblivious of her surroundings, after a while she simply fades away.

The legendary landmark once boasted 22 active ghosts and spirit sightings in the hundreds. According to a former township employee, the ethereal population includes, "Abigail and Peter, Lydia and Reverend Wilson, Captain Morgan, Robert..." The list goes on and includes a spectral British sea captain who peers through a spyglass toward the sea. Loud sobs emanate from the bedroom. This is Abigail's domain where she keeps vigil for her beloved's return with an expressionless stare. This is the same chamber where on July 4, 1975, local boys observed the sewing machine door open and the foot treadle moving according to the late paranormal researcher Hans Holzer.

Peter is Abigail's son whose phantom wears colonial-style shirt and knickers. When Gertrude Neidlinger curated the building as the Shoal Harbor Museum, Peter liked to play with the buttons that activated the interpretive displays. He enjoyed meddling with visitors' cameras as well.

Clairvoyants perceived the presence of former owner,

Reverend William Wilson performing a funeral service in front of the fireplace. They also intuit a group of men discussing maneuvers.

On a few occasions, Thomas Whitlock's spirit tagged along with visitors and went home with some of them. A former township employee said Whitlock craved attention and once accompanied her home where his spirit drove her dog crazy. From time to time, the aroma of Whitlock's pipe tobacco wafted through the air and the phantom also pilfered cigarette packs yet always put them back.

Allegedly, the notorious pirate Captain William Morgan once commandeered the house and buried treasure underneath. The bloodthirsty buccaneer transacted dirty deals at the location. His nightmarish energy bleeds into modern times. Some youngsters observed Morgan's faceless phantom draped in a hooded robe and his scary, bearded reflection in a mirror.

Psychic Jane Doherty used to conduct paranormal events on-site to educate the public and raise funds for historic preservation. The hugely successful happenings propelled the homestead to national fame. Spotlighted on the television show *Sightings*, the *U.S. News & World Report* newspaper described the Spy House as one of the three most haunted houses in America. During one séance conducted at the house, Doherty contacted a spirit named Robert who claimed to be Captain Morgan's first mate. Robert told of hidden tunnels leading from

the house to the harbor. Sonar readings substantiated the possible existence of tunnels. Doherty's intuitive impressions revealed a trapdoor used during the Revolution by George Washington, and others, when frequenting the inn. Indeed such a hatch survived where Doherty predicted. History substantiates Washington's stay across the bay in South Amboy so the story could hold water.

One evening a volunteer left the building and witnessed children playing on the grounds. After a few confusing moments he came to realize their clothes befitted an earlier era—their outmoded garb a dead giveaway to their ghostly reality.

As one visitor approached the house via Wilson Avenue, he slammed on his brakes to avoid hitting a young girl who suddenly materialized in the street. The startling delusion offered a glimpse back in time. Historic records reveal a neighborhood girl named Katie died after being run over by a horse drawn carriage. Neidlinger alleged the apparition of a little girl with a corn doll appeared from time to time on the property. Perhaps this is Katie's poor waif.

The Seabrook Wilson Homestead serves as the activity center at the Bayshore Waterfront Park. Docents conduct tours that showcase bay ecology and local history. The waterfront location affords panoramic views of the harbor and Manhattan's skyline. Dare to experience the possibility of the paranormal and perhaps gain a peek at phantom forms who figure prominently in the home's haunted history.

Clarke House Museum

500 Mercer Road
Princeton

Hugh Mercer was a soldier and physician. He became a brigadier general in the Continental Army and a close friend to George Washington. Some speculate that Mercer originated Washington's daring plan to cross the Delaware River and surprise the Hessians at the Battle of Trenton on December 26, 1776. Whatever the case, Mercer certainly contributed to its successful execution.

During the ensuing Battle at Princeton on January 3, 1777, Mercer's horse was shot from under him. Getting to his feet, British troops quickly surrounded the general. Mistaking Mercer for George Washington, the attackers ordered a surrender. Although outnumbered, Mercer drew his saber and began to defend himself. Beaten to the ground and stabbed seven times with bayonets, Mercer was left for dead.

When Washington observed Mercer's men in retreat, he entered the fray. The general rallied the troops and repelled the British regiments as Mercer lay dying on the field. Legend says General Mercer, while still impaled with bayonet, refused to leave his men in battle and was placed to rest on the trunk of a white oak tree. The tree became known as "the Mercer Oak" and is the central feature on the seal of Mercer County. Eventually carried to the field hospital in Thomas Clarke's house near the battlefield, Mercer died of his wounds and became a fallen hero and rallying symbol of the Revolution.

Today, Clarke's homestead is a museum housing the "Arms of the Revolution" exhibit. The display presents one of the largest collections of period firearms in the region. Built circa 1772, the white clapboard farmhouse stood amid 200 acres of cleared fields during the War for Independence. Damaged by musket fire, the house served as a refuge for both sides. At the time, medical treatment was rudimentary, to say the least. For instance, doctors operated without anesthesia among blood and gore. It's distressing to imagine the excruciating pain and agony endured by the wounded and dying. So many young men were maimed for life or died. Inadvertently, these make-shift hospitals turned into the crossroads of this life and the next. Embedded with intense emotional energy, it appears these residual forces are in operation at Thomas Clarke's house on the historic Princeton Battlefield.

In one of the upstairs bedrooms, custodians and visitors report discomforting feelings. The sensation of being watched and of someone disembodied brushing by them is also discerned. Sometimes unexpected shadows appear in sightseers' peripheral vision.

The gently spirited home survives where death and violence occurred. Lingering energies exist where beings met a sudden and hostile demise. Individuals may be trapped in a sort of limbo, caught between the earth plane and the next. Some, perhaps even Hugh Mercer, may not even realize they are dead. The losses at the Battle of Princeton number in the hundreds and Thomas Clarke's house continues to pulsate with the memory of the struggle.

Raritan Library

54 East Somerset Street
Raritan

"At night, here in the library, the ghosts have voices."
—ALBERTO MANGUEL

The Raritan Public Library is housed in General John Frelinghuysen's former residence. The patriarch of a prominent New Jersey family, Frelinghuysen's property comprised a larger tract purchased by Dutch settlers in 1683 from Native Americans. Built sometime before 1756, the west wing is the structure's oldest section and now serves as the children's room. The cozy space formerly functioned as a tavern, the town's meeting hall and a prison.

Originally the edifice stood as a small wooden structure bordering the Old York Road, a wilderness trail that developed into a major thoroughfare between New York and Philadelphia. In 1850, a Neo-classic portico was added to the north entrance. The four Doric columns represent Equality, Liberty, Freedom and Law. The residence also provided a welcomed respite on the Underground Railroad.

Listed on the National Register and New Jersey Register of Historic Places, former New Jersey Congressman, Peter Frelinghuysen, Jr., donated the building to the borough in 1970. Careful restoration, with attention to detail, readied the former home for use as a library and museum.

At odd times during the night, neighbors see lights go on and off in the Federal style structure. They report sightings of an elderly woman in certain windows and in the garden behind the building. After John Frelinghuysen died in 1833, two of his daughters, Sarah and Katherine, continued to live in the house. Perhaps the spirit is one of the sisters' leftover energy still lingering at the property.

On quiet mornings, staffers occasionally hear someone walking about the rooms. They disregard the sound assuming it's a co-worker until they realize they're all alone—or are they? Another phenomenon is the aroma of old-fashioned aftershave and pipe tobacco infusing the atmosphere. Additional unexplainable anomalies include sporadic opening and closing of doors and attic windows on their own.

Librarian Jackie Widows said once a terrified teenager raced down the stairs because she heard disembodied laughter. The girl ran out the front door in a panic. Ms. Widows also said a young mother grew agitated over her toddler's frightened reaction to "the man standing over there." No one except the child witnessed the man.

The janitor told his tale of hearing people talking downstairs as he worked alone in the building after hours. On occasion, even staff members hear the mysterious voices as they descend the stairs. During a 1995 renovation the door slammed shut in a room where a painter worked. When the laborer tried to exit he could not open the door and felt an invisible presence kept him trapped. Eventually, the door released; he dashed outside and never returned. A carpenter, and even certain patrons, refuse to set foot in the library. They decline to discuss the reasons why.

So when books mysteriously pop off shelves and fall to the floor in the Raritan Library, it may be an earlier tenant prompting you to remember a chapter of history exemplified by the General John Frelinghuysen House.

Ringwood Manor

1304 Sloatsburg Road
Ringwood

In 1764, handsome Peter Hasenclever charmed London society announcing riches to be made from New Jersey iron mines. He formed the American Iron Company and even persuaded Queen Charlotte, wife of King George III, to back his enterprise.

Hasenclever purchased the old iron works in Ringwood. His 535 workers opened 53 different iron mines and under the boss' direction, built forges, furnaces, roads, dams, houses, stables, bridges, reservoirs, ponds and mills. Hasenclever developed iron works at Ringwood, Charlotteburg, Long Pond (Greenwood Lake) and others in New York State. The remote Ringwood location stood as the centerpiece of his 50,000 acre iron empire.

On the downside, his ambitious expansion increased expenses and netted few dividends for investors who claimed mismanagement. Hasenclever went back to England and never returned to the Ramapo hills. Actually, maybe he did...

Some Ringwood visitors detect a distinguished looking gentleman stylishly dressed in 18th century clothing strolling the grounds. Those in the know identify the dashing spirit as Peter Hasenclever. His visage also appears in upstairs windows.

By 1771, ironmaster Robert Erskine, arrived from England. He served the nation as the first Surveyor-General during the Revolution producing more than 200 highly accurate maps. Ringwood existed between West Point and Morristown on the military road and George Washington often visited Erskine to discuss military strategy. Ringwood's iron helped to supply the Continental Army with components of the chain system used to defend the Hudson River, camp ovens and other hardware.

Erskine died in 1780. He was buried in the property's old cemetery along with more than 150 pioneers, early iron makers and Revolutionary War soldiers. According to legend, a brick popped out of his vault and Erskine's spirit escaped from the grave. When all is quiet and the mists lay low, Erskine's spirit might be discerned sitting on his tombstone swinging a lantern. His spirit also strolls the grounds (to commune with Hasenclever perhaps?) and the manor house.

In 1807, Martin J. Ryerson purchased the historic ironworks and began building the first section of the present 1810 Manor. A small, 10-room, Federal style building.

In 1853, inventor and industrialist Peter Cooper acquired the manor together with his son-in-law Abram S. Hewitt, one-time New York City mayor. Cooper and Hewitt became the major supplier of gunmetal to the Union cause during the American Civil War.

By the end of the 19th century, Ringwood no longer played a major role in the iron and steel industry. Ring-wood's iron mines closed when iron production moved West. The wealthy and influential Hewitt family trans-formed the estate into a summer retreat to include 51 rooms, 24 fireplaces and more than 250 windows. The manor is an eclectic mix of styles typical of the Victorian period.

Eleanor Hewitt remains in residence and indicates she isn't happy with strangers invading her space. To show her displeasure she relocates figurines, makes papers disappear and opens books to specific pages. Docents find lights burning when they know they've shut them off.

A former housemaid haunts a small bedroom on the second floor where she allegedly was beaten to death. Several visitors hear disembodied footsteps, heavy objects being moved and soft crying emanating from the empty room. The bedroom door often opens on its own and the bed is sometimes found rumpled.

Nebulous figures escort some after-hours guests out of the cemetery. Chiefly, a Revolutionary War soldier's specter stands guard until visitors exit the gate.

In 1938, the Hewitt family donated Ringwood Manor and its contents to the State of New Jersey. Preserved as a historic house museum and state park, Ringwood Manor and grounds exemplify Victorian wealth and lifestyle.

A ghost hunting visit to this historic relic is a must. The perfect time to witness the paranormal activity is right before a storm when energy levels peak and spark spectral shenanigans.

Steuben House

1209 Main Street
River Edge

In gratitude for his service to the Continental Army, the State of New Jersey presented Jan Zabriskie's homestead to Major-General Friedrich Wilhelm von Steuben. Confiscated from the Loyalist in 1781, this gift was one of many land grants von Steuben received from several states in gratitude for training the Continental Army. Baron von Steuben literally wrote the book that served as the standard United States drill manual until the War of 1812. The country estate bestowed upon him for his service is known as the Steuben House.

The State of New Jersey took possession of the property in 1928. The historic house was renovated and opened as a public museum exhibiting period artifacts in 1939.

In 1951, von Steuben's spirit returned for a visit. A female tourist observed him sitting in the living room. Von Steuben spoke to her in what she termed a "faraway voice" and questioned her about the Revolutionary War, George Washington and the state of the union. Von Steuben seemed quite startled when told the date and he suddenly vanished.

Olde Stone House

208 Egg Harbor Road
Sewell

*"Paranormal research is sort of like
communicating with history."*

—DOUG HOGATE, JR.

George and Susanna Morgan and their six children first resided in the 1730 limestone structure known as the Olde Stone House. According to Doug Hogate, Jr., founder of Jersey Unique Minds Paranormal Society (JUMPS), limestone is known to conduct and stimulate supernatural activity. He revealed an oft-told story of an ethereal Civil War soldier seen and heard walking down the steps inside the house.

Spirits will use any available energy source to communicate. At the Open House celebration for the 1730 structure, an invisible inhabitant flickered candle flames to show its appreciation, according to Cookie Kaizer. On another occasion, when Cookie was alone in the house she noticed the candle flame wavering. She grew sensitive to the spirit's unique ways of expression. Sure enough a knock resounded at the door—the unseen presence alerted her of someone's approach. Cookie felt certain the indiscernible specter protected her and the house.

When Cookie and a small army of volunteers worked on restoring the Olde Stone House, she felt "guided" by the spirit and even received inspiration through her dreams. Conversely, some others felt chilled to the bone when unseen fingers tousled their hair—their upset so intense they ran screaming from the house.

While weeding the herb garden, Cookie heard three taps on the window even though the house stood empty. The three knocks continued until she noticed a middle-aged, female apparition, with no discernable facial features, peering out an upstairs window. Hogate concurs about the female spirit inside the house who may have succumbed to typhoid fever.

Van Wickle House

1289 Easton Avenue
Somerset

The beautiful colonial home known as "The Meadows" was built as a wedding gift in 1752 for Evert and Cornelia Van Wickle. Five years later, the couple died when fire broke out in the house. Their bodies were the first interred on the property; the Revolutionary War dead laid to rest alongside them decades later.

A long-held superstition in many cultures cautions against unsettling the dead; once they are disturbed they will haunt forever. The couple's remains were excavated which may explain the unusual haunted history of the house.

When privately owned, some odd happenings experienced by residents included doilies flying across the room, doors opening and closing on their own and radios randomly playing full-blast at times during the day and night. The inhabitants found the spirited goings-on irritating, to say the least.

Revolutionary War soldiers supposedly still roam the hallways. In the past, resident pets would sit for hours and stare at the ceiling. What did they perceive that no human sight could? At times the dog would wag its tail while the cat hissed in reaction to an invisible presence.

Once a water puddle formed on a chair seat only moments before occupied. The source of the liquid could not be found. It's unclear why, but some ghosts do tend to leave behind wet patches. Some dwellers heard terrifying screams and felt icy touches; items disappeared and would reappear somewhere else. One night the sound of someone washing dishes, slamming pots and pans and making a general racket resounded in the unoccupied kitchen. Incessant knocking on the front door often occurred but when answered, *no one was there.*

The frustrated owner threatened the entities with burning down the house unless they stopped their antics. Afterwards, *five* forlorn apparitions appeared in his bedroom. Their identities thought to be Cornelia and Evert and three former owners. After lingering for a moment, they floated into the bathroom and faded away.

One caretaker experienced most of the eeriness of

previous tenants—disembodied door knocking, ghostly voices, ice cold touches, among other worldly weirdness. On more than one occasion, he awoke to see an apparition of a middle-aged, 18th century woman sitting at his feet.

In 1938, photographer Nathaniel R. Ewan documented the house for the Historic American Buildings Survey. In the above photo, he captured the image of a spectral child seen on the left hand side. A Van Wickle descendent perhaps?

In 1976, Franklin Township purchased the property and formed the Meadows Foundation to maintain the house as an historic site.

Ocean County Courthouse

118 Washington Street
Toms River

Ocean County's new governing body conducted their organizational meeting in May 1850 at Thomas P. Barkalow's tavern, located at Main and Water Streets in Toms River. The men voted and proclaimed Toms River the county seat over Lakehurst by one ballot.

The most impressive building in town is Greek revival style, a temple design popular during the mid-19th century. The building is constructed of bricks shipped by schooner from Haverstraw, New York and conveyed to Robbins Cove on Allen Street. Teams of horses pulled the brick-laden wagons from the riverbank to the construction site on an old cornfield.

The Court Room's history includes many community, civic and religious functions other than the courts. During the Civil War, the room was the scene of Union recruiting rallies and military drills were conducted on the lawn in front of the Courthouse steps.

In 1994, Courtroom I was beset by a series of strange occurrences. Doors knobs rattled, motion detectors went off inside vacant rooms and lights blinked on and off without cause. Most impressive was the appearance of a misty, male apparition. The spirit of a middle-aged man dressed in shirt and tie revealed himself inside the courtroom alongside a tear-shaped filmy figure.

One woman who frequents the court for business, contacted this writer after reading about the haunting in *Ghosts of the Jersey Shore*. On several occasions she's encountered the wraith in the building. Mostly she observes him walking the halls but one time he stood before her as the elevator doors opened. She said he seems to go about his business oblivious to his surroundings.

Dey Mansion

199 Totowa Road
Wayne

While the British occupied New York City, General George Washington encamped his army in the strategic Preakness Valley. The Dey Mansion sheltered Washington and his Continental Army staff officers, including Alexander Hamilton, Marquis de Lafayette, Lord Stirling and "Mad" Anthony Wayne, as they grappled with decisions affecting the outcome of the Revolutionary War.

Dirck Dey built the imposing Georgian manor house in the 1740s. His son, Theunis, went on to become a Colonel in the Bergen County Militia during the Revolutionary War.

An unsuccessful plan to capture Major General Benedict Arnold, who conspired to turn over West Point to the British, was formulated at the Dey mansion. Washington wanted Arnold captured alive. "No circumstances whatever shall obtain my consent to his being put to death," he wrote.

Today the house is owned and operated as a museum by Passaic County. The two-acre site includes several replica outbuildings, including a Blacksmith Shop and Plantation House. Guided tours transport the visitor to a remarkable era in our country's history.

Almost any aged house, especially one in which leaders struggled to achieve independence from the hands of tyranny, holds residual energy. In this case, the Dey Mansion is gently haunted. Witnesses observe strange shadows and lights. Sometimes visitors sense tension in the conference room. Staff members admit a presence expresses itself as "a gentle breeze caressing their shoulders."

Haunting activity aside, the house museum, its artifacts and documents, bring to life the achievements of the home's inhabitants during trying days when victory over oppression hung in the balance.

"So from the world of spirits there descends
a bridge of light, connecting it with this."
—HENRY WADSWORTH LONGFELLOW

Hobart Manor

300 Pompton Road
Wayne

Today the building known as Hobart Manor houses the offices of William Paterson University's president and administrative staff. The grand structure also hosts special events in the impeccably restored 19th century reception rooms.

Originally, the country estate belonged to John McCullough, a Scottish immigrant who made a fortune in the wool industry. He commissioned the castle-like structure in 1877 when the region served as a convenient getaway for city dwellers seeking recreation and solace in the Watchung Mountains.

In 1902, Jennie Tuttle Hobart, the widow of Garret Augustus Hobart, the 24th U.S. vice-president under William McKinley, purchased the manor house for her son. After an extensive renovation in 1915, which expanded the structure to a forty-room house, the Tudor-style mansion became a high society enclave. In 1941, both mother and son, Garret Jr., passed away in the house only eight months apart. Word around campus is these two spirits, and possibly others, remain in residence at the splendid manor.

In life, Jennie frequently hosted festive holiday parties and important social events. One can imagine her in this elegant home descending the grand stairway to greet her guests. College security officials maintain Jennie's spirit appears as a vague, white form on the main staircase. University employees who witnessed her apparition claim she seems to be performing her daily routine as if still alive.

According to some paranormal researchers, when the same apparition is seen doing the same things over and over, and the ghost seems oblivious to the living, this anomaly is defined as a "residual haunting." A residual haunting is a playback of past happenings. The apparitions involved may not be spirits, but "recordings" somehow imprinted on the environment. What triggers the replay of events remains a mystery.

According to Elias Zwillenberg in *New Jersey Haunts*, a former administrator who visited the building with her three-year-old son during renovations said her boy enjoyed a conversation with an old woman in a flowing white dress who he called "The Grandma." Grandma, presumed to be Jennie Hobart, expressed her unhappiness to the boy over all the workman in her house and that she was leaving until they were done.

A clairvoyant "reading" the building glimpsed a young man's spirit sitting on the staircase and reading a newspaper. Could this impression of Garret Hobart also be an imprint on the environs or is he keeping company with other family members in an alternative universe? Sightings of other Hobarts peering out the leaded glass windows are occasionally glimpsed.

Ethereal piano music sometimes emanates in the dwelling disturbing the stillness. Apparently a leftover tune of times gone by since no piano exists in the building.

Guggenheim Cottage

Cedar and Norwood Avenues
West Long Branch

Across Cedar Avenue from Shadow Lawn is the Murry and Leonie Guggenheim Cottage built where New Jersey's only vice-president, Garret A. Hobart, once lived. In 1903, Murry and Leonie Guggenheim appointed architects Carrere and Hastings, designers of the New York Public Library, to create a summer residence. The Beaux Arts building received the Gold Medal from the American Institute of Architects.

Murry Guggenheim died in 1939 but Leonie continued to summer at her West Long Branch cottage until she passed away twenty years later. Now known as the Guggenheim Library, many say Leonie's spirit glides along the grand staircase every night—her filmy, phantom witnessed by mystified campus police officers. The spirit's presence on the stairs may explain the noticeable creaking often heard as well as the perceptible drop in temperature. At night, even campus police detected a female form wearing a white gown standing at a window when the building stood empty.

Many discern a definite presence evoking unease among the library stacks. A sensitive French student became so distracted from her studies she exited the reading room because she felt certain an incorporeal entity observed her. Odd happenings occur in the computer room where cursors move on computer screens even when operators aren't near the monitors. Sometimes, inexplicable tiny triangles appear on the screens. Technicians cannot explain this mysterious glitch. From time to time, a perfume fragrance is noticeable even though workers wear no cologne.

Most astoundingly, filmmakers inadvertently captured an awesome anomaly when filming the grounds for *Shadows of Shadow Lawn.* A garden statue, who some claim to be modeled after Leonie Guggenheim, appears to blink and crack a slight smile. Expert analysis is unable to explain the uncanny movement—to see the film is to believe it.

Shadow Lawn

400 Cedar Avenue
West Long Branch

Hubert T. Parsons, president of the F.W. Woolworth Company, built Shadow Lawn in 1929. The Great Depression ruined Parsons financially and the house sold in 1939 for $100.

The structure stands on the site of an earlier estate destroyed by fire. The colonial, wooden-frame building served as the summer White House for President Woodrow Wilson in 1916. He conducted his re-election campaign from the estate utilizing the enormous porches as speaking platforms to address the crowds assembled on the expansive property.

Snubbed by society, Parson's tenancy turned into turmoil. A devastating fire destroyed the lavish home in 1927. Immediately, Parsons commissioned a new, fireproof manse. Modeled after the Palace of Versailles, the new dwelling contained 130 rooms and ranked among the top twenty mansions in America.

In its prime, the elaborate estate included a 10-room superintendent house, two-story garage, eight greenhouses, horse barn, cattle barn, poultry house, two-story palm house, bullpen, ram pen, sheep pens, pheasant pens, rabbit hutches, an icehouse, three workmen cottages and kennels for the six police dogs turned loose on the grounds every midnight. The self-sustaining enclave maintained a 100 member staff.

Hubert, his wife Maysie and her sister Bertha led a lonely existence in their sumptuous digs. Their old-moneyed neighbors snubbed the nouveau riche couple and considered them socially inept. The invitations to lavish Shadow Lawn dinner parties were routinely declined.

The 1929 stock market crash signaled a downtown in Parson's fortune and eventually the house went to auction.

Now known as Woodrow Wilson Hall, in 1956, the mansion was incorporated into Monmouth University. Featured in many architecture and art books and television commercials, Wilson Hall also served as the setting for the 1982 movie, *Annie.*

These days disembodied footsteps and pipe organ music still echo throughout the main campus building baffling all who discern the mysterious sounds. Staffers on the night shift hear indistinguishable conversations and doors opening and closing when alone in the historic hall. Most astonishing is a photo taken in the dining room sometime in the 1990s. The picture captured two transparent women dressed in maid uniforms tending to a modern day dinner party. Perhaps they were part of the Parson's staff and stayed behind waiting for the dinner guests to finally arrive.

In the Office of Special Events, an unseen presence sends chills up the spines of the workers. According to the documentary, *Shadows of Shadow Lawn,* this eerie visit only occurs during times when staffers prepare for a major event. Perhaps Mrs. Parson's spirit likes to keep her hand in planning the well-attended parties thrown these days in her earthly abode.

J. Thompson Baker House

3008 Atlantic Avenue
Wildwood

The J. Thompson Baker National Historic House is named after its former owner, a New Jersey congressman and founder of the Wildwoods. Built in 1904, President Woodrow Wilson stayed at the historic house during a campaign junket six days before his 1912 presidential election.

Baker served as the first Mayor of Wildwood and his former dwelling is now home to the Wildwood Civic

Club. The interior décor exemplifies the life-style during Baker's tenancy. Period books as well as children's toys lie scattered throughout the house as if the inhabitants still enjoyed their home. Some feel they still do.

Several civic club members avoid going into the building by themselves after dark although they can't say exactly why—*something* inside makes them feel uneasy. Some visitors to the residence heard footsteps in the foyer and on the front porch. When they looked to see who walked in the house they found no one.

The strange goings-on prompted Theresa Williams, president of the Friends of the J. Thompson Baker House, to invite the Cumberland County Paranormal research group to investigate the happenings. The ghost hunters, headed by Clay Borneman, recorded electronic voice phenomena, called EVPs for short. The group taped indistinguishable voices while recording on the staircase and also captured strange noises in the attic. A journalist reporting on the paranormal investigation observed a couple dressed in vintage clothing in his peripheral vision.

The civic club conducts historic house tours, a worthwhile expedition, and various other events throughout the year. Pay a visit to the home and see what appears in *your* line of vision...

Acknowledgements

I would like to express my sincere appreciation to the individuals who provided information. In alphabetical order these people are: Clay Borneman, Phil Calfina, Jane Doherty, Sandy Epstein, Cookie Kaizer, L'Aura Hladik, Patrick Kurdes, Elizabeth McGrath, Donald J. Peck, Arlene Pontenzone, Andrew Sandall, Jackie Widows and Theresa Williams. I truly value your assistance and contributions. I am also indebted to the many authors whose informative articles and books appear in the bibliography. I am most appreciative of the dedicated individuals who persevere to preserve New Jersey's historic houses. Many thanks to my eagle-eyed friends Tina Kush Crepezzi and Maryann Way for their review and to my creative graphic designer Deb Tremper for her patience.

Bibliography

Augenstein, Seth. "Medium leads ghost tours at historic Hermitage in Ho-Ho-Kus." *Town Journal*, October 29, 2015.

Barefoot, Daniel W. *Spirits of '76*. John F. Blair, Publisher, 2009.

Bastien, Jan Lynn. *Haunted Mount Holly*. The History Press, 2008.

Belanger, Jeff. *Encyclopedia of Haunted Places*. New Page Books, 2009.

Bice, Arlene S. *Haunted Bordentown*. Schiffer Publishing, ltd., 2008.

Chesek, Tom, "Ghosts in the House 'Turn of the Screw' at Monmouth U." *Asbury Park Press*, June 18, 2004.

DiIonno, Mark. *A Guide to New Jersey's Revolutionary War Trail*. Rutgers University Press, 2001.

"Garden State Ghosts." *Ghost Hunters*. Season 4, Episode12, June 11, 2008.

"Ghosts at the Physick Estate." Retrieved from: http://www.capemaymac.org/attractions/emlenphysickestate.html

Hand, Christopher. "Things That Go Bump In The County." *Philadelphia Inquirer*, October 26, 1988.

Hauck, Dennis William. *Haunted Places: The National Directory*. Penguin Books, 1996.

The Haunting of... Eric Mabius. Season 1, Episode 2. Biography Channel, November 3, 2012.

Heckman, Candace, "A hanged inmate, a haunted courthouse." *The Philadelphia Inquirer*, Philadelphia, PA.

Heimbuch, Jeff. *Allaire State Park.* http://theweirdusmessageboard.yuku. com.

Hladik, L'Aura. *Ghosthunting New Jersey.* Clerisy Press, 2008.

Holzer, Hans. *GHOSTS, True Encounters with the World Beyond.* Black Dog & Leventhal, 2004.

Hopkins, Amanda. "Cold Springs Ghosts." *Atlantic City Weekly,* October 17, 2012.

"Judgment Day." *Ghost Hunters,* Season 5, Episode 13, September 16, 2009.

Kelly, Kathy A. *Asbury Park's Ghosts and Legends.* Paranormal Books & Curiosities Publishing, 2010.

Kerry. "The Ghost of the River Road School House." *WEIRD NJ,* Issue #17, Bloomfield, NJ.

Lenik, Edward J. "Peter Hasenclever and the American Iron Company." *Northeast Historical Archeology,* 1974.

Lossing, Benson J. *Pictorial Field-Book of the Revolution,* Harper & Brothers, Publishers, 1853.

Macken, Lynda Lee. *Ghosts of the Garden State.* Black Cat Press, 2001.

_____. *Ghosts of the Garden State II.* Black Cat Press, 2003.

_____. *Ghosts of the Garden State III.* Black Cat Press, 2005.

_____. *Ghosts of the Jersey Shore.* Black Cat Press, 2011.

_____. *Ghosts of the Jersey Shore II.* Black Cat Press, 2014.

_____. *Haunted Cape May.* Black Cat Press, 2002.

_____. *Haunted Monmouth County.* Black Cat Press, 2014.

Martinelli, Patricia A. & Stansfield, Charles A. *Haunted New Jersey.* Stackpole Books, 2004.

_____. *The Big Book of New Jersey Ghost Stories.* Stackpole Books, 2013.

Matawan Historical Society. "Burrowes Mansion, Haunted by Matawan's Past." *Matawan-Aberdeen Patch,* October 4, 2012.

McGeorge, Wallace, M.D. "The Battle of Red Bank." Gloucester County NJ Archives Military Records, January 2, 2008.

McManus, Craig. *Ghosts of Cape May*. ChannelCraig, 2005.

Meehan, William E. Jr. *Haunted Haddonfield*. Historical Society of Haddonfield, 2002.

Mills, W. Jay. *Historic Houses of New Jersey*. J. B. Lippincott Company, 1923.

Moran, Mark & Sceurman, Mark. *Weird N.J. Your Travel Guide to New Jersey's Local Legends and Best Kept Secrets*. Sterling Publishing, 2009.

Perrotto, Patrick and Tom Hanley. *Shadows of Shadow Lawn* (DVD). Hawk TV, 2005.

Pfister, Jude M. *Morris County's Acorn Hall*. The History Press, 2015.

"Phantoms of Jersey." *Ghosts Hunters*. Season 6, Episode 4, March 24, 2010.

Rauber, Al. "Haunted Houses." Retrieved from http://www.scaryplace.com/HauntedAllaireVillage.html.

Remo, Jessica. "Spirits in the Night." *New Jersey Monthly*, September 13, 2010.

Resnick, Brian. "Long-Dead Bigamist Congressman Still Haunts South Jersey." *National Review*, October 31, 2014.

Roberts, Christine. "Paranormal investigators speak to the undead residents of the town of Historic Smithville, N.J." *New York Daily News*, October 16, 2012.

Rodia, Lauren. "Who may haunt the Olde Stone House Village in Washington Township?" NJ.com, October 20, 2015.

Smith, Hannah Whitall. *John M. Whitall: The Story of His Life*. Kessinger Publishing, 2007.

Spitz, Lisa. "Guess Who's Sleeping in Your Attic?" *Acorn*, September 30, 1983.

Stives, Ruth Calia. "Imlay House may be part of Underground Railroad." *Examiner*, May 7, 2011.

Sudol, Karen & Moore, Kirk. "Jersey Shore Haunts." *Asbury Park Press*, October 3, 2006.

"Uninvited Guests." *Ghost Hunters*. Season 6, Episode 13, September 8, 2010.

Vosseller, Bob. "Paranormalists investigate Lacey Schoolhouse Museum." *Asbury Park Press*, June 3, 2010.

Zeman, Mary Beth, "The History and Mystery of Hobart Manor." *WP: The Magazine of William Paterson University*, Wayne, NJ; Fall/Winter 1999.

Zwillenberg, Elias. *New Jersey Haunts.* Schiffer Books, 2010.

WEBSITES

Acorn Hall: http://acornhall.org

Batsto Village: www.batstovillage.org

Bergen County Historical Society: http://www.bergencountyhistory.org/Pages/steubenhsehistory.html

Borough of Allentown, NJ: www.allentownnj.org

Burrowes Mansion Museum: http://burrowesmansion.org

Crossroads of the American Revolution: www.revolutionarynj.org

Bordentown Historical Society: http://www.bordentownhistory.org/Current_Exhibits/ClaraBarton/index.html

Camden County Historical Society: http://www.cchsnj.org

Drew University: https://www.drew.edu/fomh/history

Early History of West Long Branch: www.westlongbranch.org

Garden State Ghost Hunters: www.gardenstateghosthunters.com

Gloucester County: http://www.gloucestercountynj.gov/depts/p/parks/parkgolf/redbank

Gloucester Township: http://www.glotwp.com/history

The Hermitage: www.hermitage.org.

Historic Absecon Lighthouse: http://www.abseconlighthouse.org

Historic Cold Spring Village: www.hcsv.org

Historic Smithville: www.smithvillenj.com

Historical Society of Haddonfield: http://haddonfieldhistory.org

The Historic Village at Allaire: www.allairevillage.org

Immigration Entrepreneurship: http://www.immigrantentrepreneurship.org

Jane Dougherty: www.janedougherty.com

The Lawrence Historical Society: http://www.thelhs.org

Lyndhurst Historical Society: http://www.lyndhursthistoricalsociety.org

The Meadows Foundation: http://www.themeadowsfoundation.org/van-wickle-house-1722

Metlar Bodine House Museum: http://www.metlarbodinehousemuseum.org

Mid-Atlantic Center for the Arts & Humanities: http://www.capemaymac.org

Monmouth University: www.monmouth.edu

Morristown County Tourism Bureau: https://morristourism.org

NJ Division of Parks & Forestry: http://www.state.nj.us/dep/parksandforests/historic/hancockhouse/hancockhouse-index.htm

NJ Skylands: http://www.njskylands.com/hsoxfordfurnace

Passaic County NJ: http://passaiccountynj.org

Proprietary House: http://www.theproprietaryhouse.org

Raritan Public Library: http://www.raritanlibrary.org

Ringwood Manor: http://www.ringwoodmanor.org

Smithville Mansion: http://www.smithvillemansion.org

The Stephen Crane House: www.thestephencranehouse.org

Warren County Culture & Heritage Commission: http://wcchc.org

Washington Township: http://twp.washington.nj.us/content/69/85/default.aspx

William Paterson University: http://www.wpunj.edu/university/history/hobartmanor.dot

Wikipedia: www.wikipedia.org

PHOTO CREDITS

Absecon Lighthouse, Allaire Village, Historic Cold Spring Village, Hobart Manor, Old Schoolhouse Museum, Seabrook-Wilson House, Smithville Mansion, Stephen Crane House and Thomas Budd House photos by author.

Acorn Hall by Mitchell Speert. https://upload.wikimedia.org/wikipedia/commons/a/a6/Acorn_Hall.jpg

Emlen Physick Estate by Staib. https://upload.wikimedia.org/wikipedia/commons/0/02/Emlen-physick-estate.jpg;

Metlar-Bodine House by Zeete.
https://commons.wikimedia.org/wiki/
File:Metlar-Bodine_House,_Red,_White,_and_Boom,_Piscataway,_NJ.jpg

Olde Stone House by Jerrye & Roy Klotz, MD.
https://upload.wikimedia.org/wikipedia/commons/d/d3/OLDE_STONE_VILLAGE_WASHINGTON_TOWNSHIP_HISTORIC_PRESERVATION%2C_GLOUCESTER_COUNTY.jpg

Raritan Library by Zeete.
https://upload.wikimedia.org/wikipedia/commons/f/f8/John_Frelinghuysen_House%2C_Raritan%2C_NJ_north_view.jpg

Shippen Manor by Tom Zmuda.
https://upload.wikimedia.org/wikipedia/commons/6/6e/Shippen_Manor%2C_Oxford_NJ_author_Tom_Zmuda.JPG
All files are licensed under the Creative Commons Attribution-Share Alike 3.0 Unported license.

Books by Lynda Lee Macken

Adirondack Ghosts
Adirondack Ghosts II
Adirondack Ghosts III
Array of Hope, An Afterlife Journal
Empire Ghosts, New York State's Haunted Landmarks
Ghost Hunting the Mohawk Valley
Ghostly Gotham, Haunted History of New York City
*Ghosts of Central New York
Ghosts of the Garden State
Ghosts of the Garden State II
Ghosts of the Garden State III
Ghosts of the Jersey Shore
Ghosts of the Jersey Shore II
Haunted Baltimore
Haunted Cape May
Haunted History of Staten Island
Haunted Houses of New Jersey
Haunted Houses of the Hudson Valley
Haunted Lake George
Haunted Lake Placid
Haunted Long Beach Island
Haunted Long Island
Haunted Long Island II
Haunted Monmouth County
Haunted New Hope
Haunted Salem & Beyond

*(originally published as *Leatherstocking Ghosts*)

BLACK CAT PRESS
www.lyndaleemacken.com

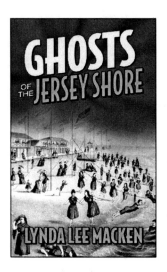

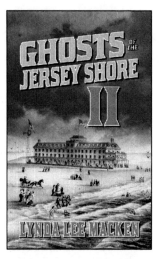

BLACK CAT PRESS
www.lyndaleemacken.com

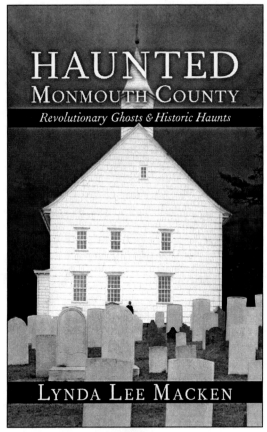

HAUNTED
MONMOUTH COUNTY
Revolutionary Ghosts & Historic Haunts

LYNDA LEE MACKEN

CPSIA information can be obtained
at www.ICGtesting.com
Printed in the USA
FFOW01n2334030418
46152344-47315FF